Erica Wilson's
BRIDES BOOK

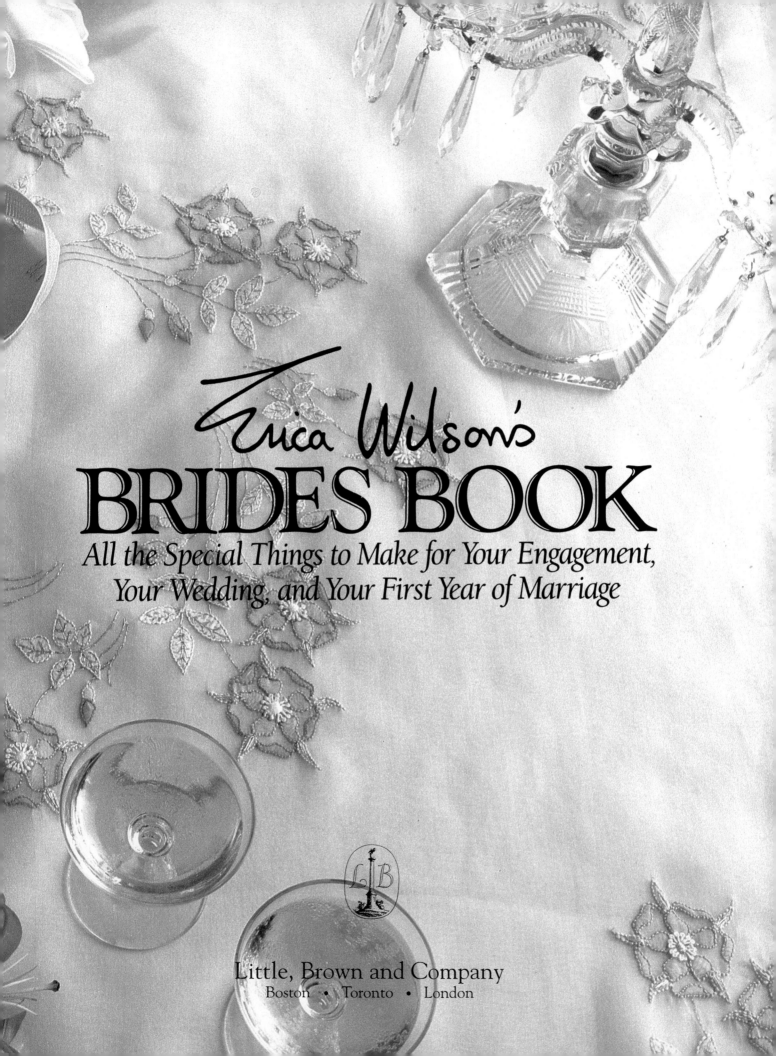

Erica Wilson's
BRIDES BOOK

All the Special Things to Make for Your Engagement,
Your Wedding, and Your First Year of Marriage

Little, Brown and Company
Boston • Toronto • London

FIRST EDITION

Library of Congress Cataloging-in-Publication Data
Wilson, Erica,
(Brides book)
Erica Wilson's brides book: all the special things to make for your
engagement, your wedding and your first year of marriage.
p.   cm.
1. Needlework—Patterns. 2. Weddings. 3. Gifts. I. Title.
II. Title: Brides book.
TT753. W55   1989
746.4—dc 19   88-26701
ISBN 0-316-94481-5

Produced by Allen D. Bragdon Publishers, Inc.
Printed in Hong Kong through Bookbuilders Ltd.

10   9   8   7   6   5   4   3   2   1

Published simultaneously in Canada
by Little, Brown & Company (Canada) Limited

ACKNOWLEDGEMENTS

Grateful thanks to the following companies and individuals for their supplies and models:

Vogue/Butterick Company
CM Offray & Son Inc.
Husquanna/Viking Sewing Machine Company
Illinois Bronze Paint Company
Stacey Fabrics Corporation

Anne Humphries: For her inspiration on Scrap
    Art Pillows
Mrs. Glebe Thompson: Appliqué Shorts
Dorothy Martin: Wedding Invitation Pillow
Lydia Gordon: Antique dresses
Ann H. Shetler: Wedding Favors
Janet Akhtarshenas: Padded Satin Hanger,
    Ribbon & Lace Garter, Ring Bearer's Pillow,
    Moss Heart Wreath, Kitchen Magnets,
    Christmas Ornaments
Rachel Pelman/Michael Flores–The Old
    Country Store: Country Bride Quilt
Ellie Schneider/Maria Filosa courtesy of CM
    Offray & Son: Bridal Fan, Headdress ribbons
Phoebe Hart Roper: Animal Rug

All designs not listed above are the author's
original work.

MODELS:
Vanessa Kagan
Anne M. Lingerman
Matthew J. Diserio
Whiting K. Willauer, Jr.
Emmy Higgins
Lewis Nash
Caroline Ledbetter (flower girl)

PHOTOGRAPHERS
Lilo Raymond
Joshua Greene
Vladimir Kagan

STYLISTS
Elizabeth Varney
Vanessa Kagan
Alicia Beldegreen

EDITING
Allen D. Bragdon
Judith Rubin

ART DIRECTION
John B Miller

Photography at: Petticoat Row, Nantucket, MA;
Nantucket house of Mr. & Mrs. Dan de
Menocal; Nantucket house of Mrs. John Rhodes

TABLE OF CONTENTS

THE COMFORTS OF HOME

THE FIRST YEAR'S CELEBRATIONS

ALPHABET OF TECHNIQUES & STITCHES

WEDDING INVITATION PILLOW
(Shown on following page)

This beautiful satin pillow will become a treasured heirloom and an elegant reminder of the joyous days of preparation. (p. 66)

Mr. and Mrs. Gerald G. Westerhausen

request the honour of your presence

at the marriage of their daughter

Andrea

to

Russell William Nynas

Saturday, the nineteenth of October

Nineteen hundred and eighty-five

at five o'clock

Trinity Episcopal Church

Findlay, Ohio

*Y*our wedding day
symbolizes a new beginning: two people
coming together in love to share their lives,
working side by side to build a foundation of traditions
that will be passed on from generation to generation.
In the early American West, couples built their homes, and then
with the work of their own hands furnished them. Times have hardly
changed. Today's couples work together and share financial commitments,
household chores, child rearing and plans for their future. In recent years,
our appreciation for all things handmade has become a national passion. More
than ever before, we long to create heirlooms that will be passed along with our
traditions. And what better time to begin than for your wedding day? Your own
handiwork can reflect your personal commitment to each other in a time-honored
fashion. Drawing on all the rich traditions of needlework through the ages, this book
will show you how you can create a romantic array of special things for your engagement,
your trousseau and the wedding day itself, as well as for your first home and all the
celebrations and holidays of your first year of marriage. There is nothing to equal the
satisfaction of creating with your own two hands, and in these pages you will find ideas from the
simplest to the most sophisticated. For instance, you can learn how to make delicate beaded lace
for your own wedding gown—or, as easily as ABC, make ribbon roses for your headdress or party
favors for your reception. This book has four main themes. "Before the Wedding" offers ideas
for your hope chest and everything to fill it—towels and pillowcases, quilts and sachets. You can
make romantic lingerie and a pretty bag to keep it tidy. And let's not forget gifts for the
groom—perhaps a handknit sweater, a stenciled sweatshirt or a needlepoint belt, so that he is
enchanted with your handiwork at the very outset! Then for the great day itself come all those
wonderful things to make the wedding complete. The wedding dress can be simply embellished
with beaded lace, or made complete with lace collage and tulle or white-on-white embroidery.
And, to complete your bride's ensemble, you can create an original headdress, beaded shoes, fan
and satin prayerbook cover. There are dresses for bridesmaids and flower girl, and, of course, all
the magical touches for the occasion—the ring bearer's pillow, a tie and cummerbund for the
groom, party favors and a tablecloth fit for the wedding cake at the reception. In "The
Comforts of Home," you'll find a collection of special creations large and small for your first
home together. Working with fabrics, quilting, cross stitch and needlepoint, and choosing
beautiful color schemes for each room, you can craft charming and practical handworked
things for your bedroom, bath, kitchen and living room. Finally, there are the
celebrations and holidays through the first year: Valentine's Day, Easter,
Independence Day, Thanksgiving, his birthday, your first Christmas together. There
are two projects for commemorating your first anniversary: You can make a
wedding sampler to treasure in unusual needlepoint cross-stitch lace, inspired
by a rare piece of point d'Alençon lace in the Metropolitan Museum of
Art, and a beautiful lace-covered photo album to store your precious
memories. Whether the projects you select are simple or
intricate, they will become your very own heirlooms and
traditions of tomorrow. Make them with love, share
them in happiness, and finally entrust them to
your future generations.
—*Erica Wilson*

BEFORE THE WEDDING

From the moment you become engaged, your handiwork can celebrate all the happy anticipation of the day to come. Here are very special gifts to make for him, and a stenciled hope chest to fill with a trove of treasures for your new life together.

STENCILED HOPE CHEST & COUNTRY BRIDE QUILT
(Shown on previous page)

A hope chest was the traditional way for a bride to store the quilts and linens she had been stitching since she was a young girl, in preparation for her future marriage. The chest itself makes a handsome and useful piece of furniture today. It can serve as a coffee table, a concealment for stereo equipment, and of course as storage for winter blankets, sweaters and extra pillows. The stenciling technique, using acrylic paints, is effective and easy. (p. 66)

Start your trousseau with the romantic motifs of the Country Bride Quilt. In earlier times, hearts were not to be taken lightly, or used on anything but a bride's bed, lest they bring about a broken romance. For this appliquéd quilt done in soft pastels, you might use pinks or blues, calicoes or ginghams. (p. 67)

PINWHEEL SCRAP QUILT

Patchwork, with every piece of equal tone-value, is the hallmark of scrap quilting. The overall design almost disappears in a kaleidoscope of harmonious shades. This is a classic quilt for your hope chest and an excellent beginner's quilt to learn different ways of piecing. (p. 69)

SCRAP ART PILLOWS

Transform leftover fabrics into objects worthy of your trousseau, by using the popular scrap art style of patchwork. The most attractive designs are made with colors of equal tone-value, to give the finished design an overall color balance without strong contrasts. Today, you can buy fabric in antique mini-print calicoes and Provençal prints like the ones from the '30s, or you can stick to the original idea and use scraps; discarded neckties, for instance, make beautiful scrap art designs.

These hand- or machine-appliquéd pillows are so simple, you can make several in an afternoon. (p. 71)

STENCILED FLOWER QUILT

Your color scheme is as free as your imagination when you stencil a quilt. A light brushstroke or stippling can be enhanced later with embroidery. When each finished square is quilted and pieced, the effect is distinctive and charming. (p. 70)

esign personalized, appealing bedspreads, linens, placemats, towels and even sweaters, as items for your hope chest and as gifts for your loved ones, using the graceful alphabet and colorful birthday flowers shown on the sampler. Employing the marvelously foolproof technique described in the instructions, combine the motifs and work your embroidery in white on white or color with simple stitches (see next page). Birthday flowers are, from left to right, carnation (January); violet (February); jonquil (March); daisy (April); lily of

15

the valley (May); rose (June); larkspur (July); poppy (August); aster (September); cosmos (October); chrysanthemum (November) and holly (December). (p. 72)

RIBBON & LACE BRIDAL PILLOWS

Marie Antoinette of France and Queen Anne of England wore dresses stitched with fine silk ribbons. Today, Queen Anne embroidery (shown here on the right- and left-hand pillows) is done with narrow ribbons made especially for this type of embroidery. The stitching is accented with white beads, ivory floss and snowy pearl cotton.

The pink pillow (center), with its mock lace effect, is worked on Aida cloth in cross stitch using two weights of cotton floss. Finished with a simple eyelet border, these pillows add a delicate elegance to your bridal bed. (pp. 74–76)

DREAMY NIGHTDRESSES

A length of filmy fabric becomes a demure, romantic nightdress, smocked with simple stitches in bands around the top. The fine, hand-rolled hem at top and bottom, whipstitched in the same color as the smocking, completes a negligeé fit for a bride.

The top of the nightdress on the right is cut from a handkerchief in delicate white-on-white embroidery, and the seams are done in French point de Paris, forming a row of openwork holes, a charming touch. (p. 76)

TAP PANTS

Fun to wear and distinctly feminine, these open-leg French pants are embroidered in satin stitch and edged with lace. Point turc, a double row of openwork holes, forms a perfectly flat seam at center front and back. Make your tap pants from the pattern given, or embellish a pair of purchased ones with your special stitchery. (p. 77)

LINGERIE BAG

A feminine organdy bag with organza ribbons is a lovely way to keep small things tidy and snag-free in a drawer. The ribbon roses are a joy to make—as if by magic, they just appear as you release the folded ribbon you have twisted in your fingers. (p. 78)

CODE FLAG BELT

Send a secret message to the man you love in a code flag belt. Spell out his name in nautical code flags, worked on needlepoint canvas in heraldic colors. (p. 79)

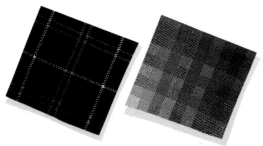

NEEDLEPOINT SLIPPERS

Warm your future husband's feet with this luxurious needlepoint gift, evoking snug images of domestic comfort. Worked in a solid, basic color or a natty plaid pattern, the firm stitching, like woven tapestry, is both handsome and hard-wearing. If you like, add his initials to the design, using the alphabet on page 72. (p. 80)

TIE CASE

This perfect gift for your groom to bring away on your honeymoon will keep his ties impeccably organized for years to come. Even a novice stitcher will find this project easy to make. The black moiré case is fully lined with a contrasting color and the covered buttons add a professional touch. (p. 80)

HIS & HER SWEATERS

A perfect pair, slightly different but a beautiful blend. Wear them together and everyone will know you were made for each other. These easy-fitting fair isle sweaters are fun to make. The charted design is simple to follow for hand or machine knitters. (p. 81)

STENCILED SWEATSHIRTS

His and her sweatshirts are a quick and wonderful way to say "we're engaged." An ordinary purchased top becomes unique when you stencil on your favorite things, using fast-drying, permanent acrylic paint. (p. 82)

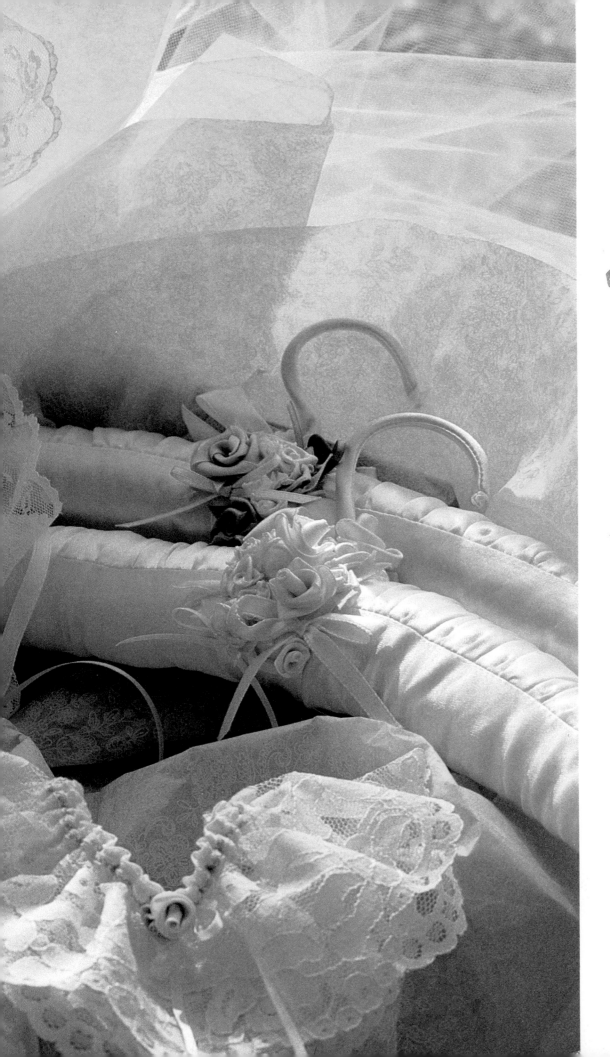

THE WEDDING

Celebrate
the day
with your own
handiwork,
from little
adornments
and party favors
to a bevy
of gowns
for the bride
and her
attendants.

SATIN HANGER, LACE GARTER &
RING BEARER'S PILLOW
(Shown on previous page)

Something old, something new, something borrowed, something blue—here is a collection of keèpsakes to enhance your wedding day that you will cherish forever. A padded hanger adorned with ribbon roses will keep your gown hanging in luxury. The ring bearer's pillow has ribbon roses and a satin heart; woven ribbons and more roses add a touch of blue to the lace garter. (pp. 83–84)

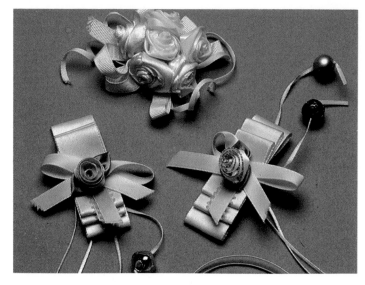

PRAYER BOOK COVER
BOOKMARKS & HAIRCLIPS

Take your wedding vows holding a prayer book beautifully covered in satin, silk and pearls. The surprising simple stitchery looks intricate. You can also make a beautiful bookmark, to accompany your prayer book and open it automatically at the right page. The handmade hairclips, adorned with ribbon roses and streamers, will make your flower girl the picture of charm. All these projects are made principally of ribbon—versatile, adaptable and wonderfully easy to use. (pp. 84–86)

BRIDE'S HANKY/
CHRISTENING BONNET

From bride's hanky to christening bonnet or vice versa, this tradition is a lovely one to pass on. If you received a bonnet as a baby you can snip the stitches and carry the hanky as "something old." Or, reverse the cycle and make the hanky first, and carry it as "something new." Make it by enhancing a beautiful linen square with embroidery and lace, or leave it plain, with Quakerish simplicity. After the wedding, tuck it away until the time comes to pass it on as a christening bonnet to the next generation. (p. 86)

I'm just a little hanky
As square as square can be
But with a tiny stitch or two
A bonnet I will be

Worn home from the hospital
Or on the christening day
And after that so neatly pressed
Then safely packed away

And so upon her wedding day
As we have oft been told
The well dressed bride must always wear
A little something old

Then what could be more fitting
Than to search out little me
And with a few fine stitches snipped
A wedding hanky be.

EMBROIDERED ORGANDY
TABLECLOTH

Shadow work on organdy with cotton floss and silver metal thread will set off the cake to perfection and grace special occasions after the wedding. Worked on the reverse side in close herringbone stitches, shadow work is a great deal easier than the delicacy of the stitching suggests. The pastel colors are surprisingly bright and create a soft, shadowy look on the right side when the tablecloth is reversed. Afterward, the cloth will be a wonderful reminder of the wedding, every time it is used. (p. 86)

28

FANCY FAVORS

Handmade favors such as almonds nestled in satin rosebuds, heart-shaped soaps wrapped in lace and sachets filled with rice make keepsakes for your attendants and decorative touches for your reception. (pp. 87–88)

SMOCKED DRESS FOR THE
FLOWER GIRL

Your flower girl will be a princess in this adorable
dress, smocked with a difference. Embroidered
ribbons are woven through the smocking, and
some of the gathering is done on the reverse side
to hold the folds in place invisibly behind bands of
decorative stitching. (p. 89)

BLOOMING BOW TIE & CUMMERBUND

And why shouldn't the groom have a little color for the occasion? In the traditions of earlier times, his costume was handstitched and as decorative as his bride's. A bouquet of satin-stitch flowers, in bright or pastel shades, can be easily added to a ready-made bow tie and cummerbund. (p. 91)

FLOWERED HEADDRESS
EMBROIDERED SHOES
& SLIPPERS

Simple stitches and careful attention to detail will help make your wedding memorable. A frothy headdress adorned with ribbon roses, beads and streamers, plus a pair of ballet slippers decorated with enchanting little flower buds, will make your bride's array unique. Precious floral motifs, delicately handstitched

onto detachable fabric bows, or applied directly to shoe toes, will transform a pair of inexpensive shoes into a set of princess's pumps. (pp. 91–92)

The technique used in the Crewel Point™ rug pictured is shown again in the swan pillow on p. 51.

ETHEREAL BRIDAL FAN

A lace fan decorated with ribbon roses, ivy leaves and baby's breath can serve beautifully in place of the bridal bouquet and become a lasting keepsake of your wedding day. Make it as shown here in white on white, or in pastels to add a touch of color to your bride's ensemble—silk ribbons for the roses are available in gold and silver and a rainbow of pale hues. (p. 92)

LACE COLLAGE YOKE

Lace appliquéd on net in the Victorian tradition takes on a completely new look when dyed in muted shades, such as stonewashed blue, pastel green or caramel. Choose a suitable dress pattern and add this collar as the perfect finishing touch. The bodice and skirt of the dress shown were made of handkerchief linen and the entire dress was dyed after the sewing was finished, creating a lovely soft look for a bridesmaid. (p. 93)

WHITE-ON-WHITE EMBROIDERED BRIDAL GOWN

One-of-a-find antique dresses have a unique loveliness—a perennial beauty. Perhaps you will be fortunate enough to find an entire period dress to fit you. Or, you can make one yourself in the same style; make this gown with high neck and pleated skirt; adding rich embroidery, follow the design given, or embellish it with a lace collage made from remnants of antique embroidered lawn. The embroidery techniques are not as difficult as you may think; a little time and patience will create a gown of lasting beauty. (p. 94)

SHADOW-STITCH EMBROIDERY FOR YOUR BRIDAL GOWN

Bell sleeves, hand-embroidered in a frosty white shadow-stitch leaf pattern, as shown on the gown at right and on next page, will augment your dress with softness and elegance. Shadow work is done

with delicate stitching on the reverse side of sheer organdy or lawn. You may restrict the embroidery to the sleeves, or extend it over the bodice. White on white is the traditional way of working shadow stitch, but once you have mastered it, for a different special look you may prefer to add a touch of color or silver as on the organdy tablecloth pictured on page 28. (p. 96)

BEADED LACE FOR YOUR BRIDAL GOWN

Tiny pearls and mother-of-pearl sequins sewn to lace appliqué on a satin gown catch the light and shimmer as the bride moves. After you've appliquéd lace to your chosen gown, you may enrich it with pearl beads in different sizes, following the contours of the lace. Or, you can apply already-beaded lace to the bottom of the finished gown, and then add the sequins to decorate the bodice, making your dress sparkling and regal. (p. 97)

PEARL-TOUCHED BRIDAL ENSEMBLE

A taffeta wedding dress, adorned with pearls stitched along its very edge, a padded, wrapped-pearl headdress and matching pumps or slippers dressed with glistening pearl knots will make your bridal ensemble one of classic simplicity. The dress pattern features an elegant low back—the bride is seen almost more that way than from the front at the wedding ceremony. Although these handwork techniques are the easiest of all the ones shown for bridal gowns, used on an exquisite fabric they can result in one of the most beautiful dresses. Also shown are the embroidered ballet slippers, described on p. 32. (pp. 97–98)

FORMAL LACE GOWN WITH TRAIN

Finish an exquisite gown with beaded lace and a regal train. To help you enjoy dancing at your wedding, a detachable bow of the train fabric allows the train to be gathered into a bustle after the marriage ceremony. Add more back interest to your gown by enhancing it with a row of tiny buttons, as pictured—actually made to be done and undone—no cheating! (p. 98)

THE COMFORTS OF HOME

Turn your first home together into an intimate retreat. These charming and practical projects will add pleasure to each day and become tomorrow's heirlooms.

WELCOME MAT
(Shown on previous page)

A portrait of your first house—or your dream house—in primitive style, with perhaps an allegorical garden surrounding it, is a foil for your crewel stitches worked on top of the needlepoint. You will enjoy "gardening" with buttonhole stitch, bullion stitch and French knots. (p. 99)

STRAWBERRIES RIPE

This appetizing toaster cover is cross stitched on a printed fabric. Normally, counted cross stitch is worked from a graph on even-weave fabric only, but the simple and ingenious method used here makes it possible on any fabric. (p. 100)

KITCHEN MAGNETS

Notes, recipes and shopping lists will be organized and eye-catching when hung on your refrigerator door with these whimsical kitchen magnets. Made in colors to coordinate with your kitchen, the magnets can be cut out, stitched, stuffed and put to work in a jiffy. (pp. 101–102)

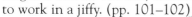

TEA COSY COTTAGE

Every house needs a teapot—the tea tastes so much better—and if you have a teapot you need a tea cosy to keep it warm. Paint the doors and windows, embroider the garden, then pad and stitch the cottage in bright calicoes. The chimney doubles as a handle, convenient for lifting the cosy on and off. (p. 102)

MOSS HEART WREATH

A moss heart to hang on any door will welcome guests and delight the eye. (p. 103)

PILLOW, BEANBAG TRAY & BOLSTER

Oversized bed pillows with a quilt or duvet are today's decorative and practical bed coverings. Add a frilled bolster and covered bed tray, and your bedroom will have a casual elegance. You can use pre-printed fabric or sheets, or stencil your own fabric with the design shown. The beanbag base is ideal for the covered tray, as it prevents slipping or spilling. The fabric on the tray is first sprayed with fabric stiffener and then sealed with a coat of clear polyurethane. (pp. 104–105)

TRAY WITH HANGER

Hanging a tray on the wall or from a shelf with hand-quilted bands of fabric, a European technique, is a decorative way to show off your handiwork. (p. 105)

RAMBLING ROSES

Do you dream of a rose-covered cottage? This one, realistically "painted" in needlepoint or cross stitch, will bring the blooms of Nantucket to your own first home, wherever you may live. Stitch it as is, following the outlined design, or substitute a portrait of your own first home. (p. 106)

SWAN PILLOW

The technique of Crewel Point™ is a special blend of crewel and bargello stitching on needlepoint canvas. Using six strands of different shades in the needle at one time produces the softly blended halo of color surrounding the swan. Pictured here on a large pillow, this speedily-stitched design is also eminently suitable for a rug such as the one shown on p. 33. (p. 107)

GATHER YE ROSEBUDS

Crewel-stitched roses are splendid as a picture or a pillow for your new home. Mastering the long and short stitch technique takes some practice, but allows you to blend colors with needle and thread as an artist handles paint and brush. (p. 108)

VICTORIAN ROSES RUG

Blooming roses are captured here on a rug in gros point. Four hands make this project fly, so you might encourage your husband to join in the stitching. Two people can easily work at one time, since the rug is made in squares later joined invisibly between geometric borders. Each rose is shaded with five colors and its position is changed in each square, so that although the design is identical, each square looks interestingly different. (p. 109)

THE FIRST
YEAR'S
CELEBRATIONS

No matter
how often you
have enjoyed
holidays with
your family,
there is a
whole new
excitement in
celebrating
together in
your very own
home.

HEIRLOOM TREASURES FOR YOUR CHRISTMAS TREE
(Shown here and on previous page)

Holiday magic shines through the windows of miniature saltbox houses. Each is cut out of cardboard, covered with fabric, then assembled with a tiny Christmas light in the center. Scallop shells glued to tiny Christmas lights create a soft Nantucket glow; baskets woven of gold ribbon ties hold baby's breath, candies or tiny gifts.

To make festive red and gold ribbon globes, blow up balloons of various sizes and glue ribbons to them. When dry, the ribbons hold the shape without the balloons. Instead of using ribbon, you can make snowy balls with lace, or alternate ribbon and lace together.

Tiny stitched pillows can be initialed and dated to mark your first Christmas together. Stuff them with sweet-smelling pine needles from your first tree and pack them away until next year, when they'll revive happy memories. (pp. 111-112)

VALENTINE'S DAY SAMPLER
Tickle your Valentine with this special cross-stitch pillow declaring, "You're no bunny till some bunny loves you." (p. 112)

EASTER PLEASERS

Make your Easter table festive with a duck bun-warmer in quilted white cotton fabric. Pad the wings and secure the padding with (naturally!) feather stitch, then line the body with bright yellow calico to match the beak. (p. 114)

Knitted kittens of brushed wool, couched in a little basket, are so adorable you won't be able to resist making them as an alternative to Easter bunnies. Knit them, join and stuff them, brush them until fluffy, then add eyes in felt, whiskers of dental floss and gingham bow ties. (p. 115)

HIS BIRTHDAY SHORTS

Make him something just for fun. A pair of shorts with appliqué inspired by all of his favorite activities and possessions will express his individuality and appeal to his sense of humor. Embroidery accents the appliqué, and words can be added for a further personal touch. (p. 115)

4TH OF JULY
PATCHWORK PICNIC BLANKET

Simple squares in patchwork make an alfresco picnic blanket. A quilt can also serve as a great picnic tote, when you tie up the four corners like a hobo bag. Use red, white and blue calico for Independence Day celebrations, or choose colors that will blend with the color scheme of your new home. This quilt, with its vivid diagonal diamond stripes, will add a graphic, colorful touch to any room. (p. 116)

THANKSGIVING TRAPUNTO PILLOW

A harvest pillow or wall hanging welcomes friends and family to your hame at Thanksgiving. The raised trapunto has a monochromatic effect just as popular in early American days as the pressed glass grapes which could have been the inspiration for this beautiful pattern from the Smithsonian Institution. Outline the harvest basket design in a shade darker than the fabric, then pad from the reverse side. (p. 116)

You are cordially invited
to join our celebration of Thanksgiving
at
two in the afternoon on November 24th
14 Sheepshead Lane, North Dennis

FIRST ANNIVERSARY SAMPLER

Celebrate the occasion of your first year together with an anniversary sampler. Designed after a rare piece of 17th-century point d'Alençon lace in the Metropolitan Museum of Art, the sampler is worked on earth-tone canvas, with the design stitched in creamy white candlewick floss. The lace border is worked in cross stitch, leaving the background open. Compare this intriguing effect of lace in needlepoint with the pink pillow shown on page 17. (p. 117)

ANNIVERSARY PHOTO ALBUM

Transform a simple album into a precious volume
to hold the cherished photographs of your wedding
day. The album is padded and covered with lace,
then silky ribbon roses and bows are added for
color and texture. (p. 118)

WEDDING INVITATION PILLOW

(Photo on p. 8)

Your printed wedding invitation
Satin fabric, 1 yard
Artist's stretcher strips
Ruffled lace trim, 1 yard
Muslin backing, superfine
   lightweight
Fabric paint and fine brush

Quilting needle and thread
Quilt batting
Six-strand cotton embroidery
   floss (optional)
Embroidery hoop and needle
   (optional)

1. Using a photocopy process, transfer printed invitation to center of satin fabric. Stretch printed fabric on artist's stretcher strips (see p. 126), marking center in both directions with basting stitches. Trace design outline (see p. 126). One-quarter of actual-size design is shown below. Duplicate exactly on each corner of fabric, or make slight variations as in pillow pictured.

2. With a fine dry brush and fabric paint (no water), paint roses and leaves in pastel pinks and greens. When paint is dry (almost immediately), baste batting and muslin behind design.

3. Using quilting needle and thread, work quilting (running) stitches closely around each leaf and flower (see p. 123 for quilting tips). If desired, using cotton floss, add embroidery details such as french knots in center of flowers and stem stitch stems. (see p. 119 for stitches). Trim and mount pillow (see p. 123).

 *The Xerox Trans Seal 300J prints the image on an extremely thin film, which can then be heat-transferred permanently onto the fabric. Photocopy services can provide you with this film, which you can then transfer yourself, using a hot iron, but it is also possible to have the whole process done for you by machine relatively inexpensively. Images heat-transferred onto polyester fabric hold indefinitely; images transferred to natural-fiber fabric fade with time and washing. (It is interesting that Talbot, who discovered photography in England, was a great friend of John Mercer, who invented mercerized cotton. Therefore, the first photograph ever printed on cloth was probably made as early as 1840.)*

WEDDING INVITATION PILLOW

Actual–size embroidery design

STENCILED HOPE CHEST

(Photo on p. 10)

Wooden chest
Furniture stripper and stain/var-
   nish (optional)
Sandpaper
Brown paper
Acrylic paints
Household sponges
Scissors
Clear polyurethane and brush
Cardboard (optional)
Batting (optional)
Fabric, any color
Glue or Velcro™ (optional)

1. Start by finding an antique or modern wooden chest with graceful lines. If necessary, strip and stain or varnish it. Roughen surfaces slightly with sandpaper so that you can work on a non-slippery surface. Cut up ordinary household sponges into simple, pleasing shapes, such as the ones shown.

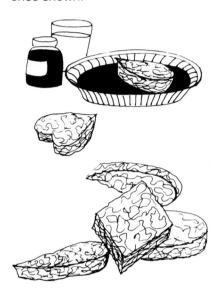

2. Work out your stenciling design: Cover one side of the chest with brown paper, taped in place. Using the sponges and paint as below (see step 4), test-stencil shapes on the paper until you arrive at a design you like.

3. Mix the acrylic paints with just a little water in a saucer. Dip the sponge shapes into the paint so they absorb the mixture thoroughly. Using your brown paper pattern as a guide, press the sponges lightly on the surface of the chest to give the paint a slightly uneven, country effect. Rinse the sponges thoroughly with water when you change colors. The paint dries almost immediately. Finish your stenciled chest with a coat of clear polyurethane.

4. If desired, after the polyurethane dries, line the chest interior: Cut pieces of thin cardboard to fit inside base, sides and lid. Cover cardboard pieces with batting, then wrap with fabric, securing fabric to reverse side of cardboard with tape. With glue or Velcro, attach cardboard pieces to chest with the padded side out.

Trica *The design on the chest pictured was inspired by the Country Bride Quilt (p. 10). Simple shapes make the best patterns; the checkerboard on the sides of the chest was made from a single square-cut sponge.*

COUNTRY BRIDE QUILT
(Photo on page 10).

100% cotton batiste in white, gingham and calico prints
Trace Erase™ pen
Quilt batting
Quilting thread, natural-color
Quilting needle
Quilt binding

Trica *Color scheme is easiest to maintain if you stick to all pinks, all blues, all golds, etc.*

1. Enlarge and transfer (see p. 126) appliqué bird design to fit inside five 20" fabric squares with a 1" border all around, and horizontally inside one 20" x 60" rectangle for pillow sham. The quilt pictured alternates five appliqué squares with four plain squares, plus pillow sham and border. Cut paper patterns of each shape shown below for appliqué.

2. Pin appliqué shapes to appropriate color fabric, placing so grain of appliqué fabric will run in same direction as grain of background fabric once the two are stitched together (fig. A). Cut out each shape leaving ¼" turnbacks (fig. B). Outline each shape with staystitching ¼" from the edge.

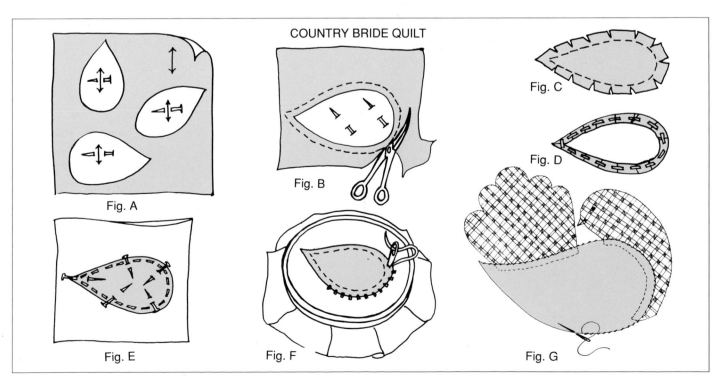

COUNTRY BRIDE QUILT

Fig. A

Fig. B

Fig. C

Fig. D

Fig. E

Fig. F

Fig. G

Clip curves, turn, press and baste turnbacks to wrong side of fabric (figs. C & D).

3. Outline design with Trace Erase™ pen on each square of fabric. Position and pin each appliqué piece to its background (fig. E); sew down with tiny stitches made at right angles to edges (fig. F). Where shapes will overlap, such as petals and bird's wing, do not fold back turnbacks; leave flat; raw edges will be covered by overlapping piece;final effect will be smoother (fig. G).

4. Embroider details: French knot eyes, straight stitch beaks, stem stitch stems (see p. 119 for stitches). Complete five appliqué squares; alternating with plain squares, assemble as shown; join pillow sham to assembled squares. Cut three 40"-wide strips of fabric to desired depth for hem

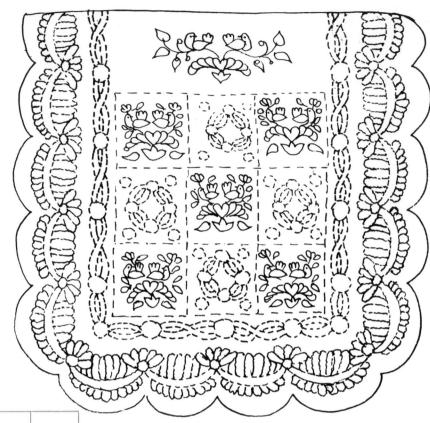

COUNTRY BRIDE QUILT   Fig. H

Appliqué designs

PINWHEEL SCRAP QUILT

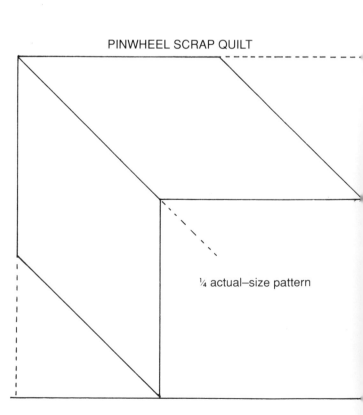

¼ actual–size pattern

and sides of quilt; join to three sides of quilt (fig. H).

5. Mark border and plain squares for quilting designs, using those shown (fig. H) or substituting your own. Baste batting and lining behind design; with quilting thread, quilt around each design and on all lines (see p. 123 for quilting tips). Finish quilt with binding, doubled for strength..

PINWHEEL SCRAP QUILT

(Photo on p. 12)

Finished size: Each block is
  11 ¼" x 11 ¼", including ¼"
seam allowances
Adhesive acetate or medium-to-
heavy cardboard
100% cotton fabrics: 6 yards solid
blue for backing and binding, 3
yards coordinating print for
piecing strips, assorted prints
for blocks
Matching sewing thread
Ruler

Marking pencil
Erasable marker
Dressmaker's carbon
Six-strand cotton embroidery
  floss, four skeins dark blue or
  desired color
Embroidery needle
Polyester batting

Trica Directions given are for a full-sized quilt, as pictured, made of 42 blocks; make fewer blocks if you want a smaller quilt. This project may be hand- or machine-stitched.

1. Transfer actual-size patterns for templates to acetate or cardboard (see p. 126). Patterns given do not include seam allowances. For hand-piecing, cut templates without seam allowances; trace around template to get exact stitching line, and cut freehand, ¼" beyond that line, for seams. For machine-piecing, cut templates with seam allowances to get exact cutting line; you can then keep the pressure foot on outer edge of fabric, using edge as a guide for keeping seams accurate.

2. Stitch pieces together with right sides facing. Each block is composed of three random prints in colors of equal depth. You may choose to use the same three prints throughout or a different grouping for each block.

3. Working one block at a time,

piece together (see figs. A and B for placement and refer to circled numbers for sequence in which seams should be stitched). For strength, do not press seams open; press them alternately to one side or the other. Press each block after it is finished, pressing dark seams away from light areas so that color will not show through.

4. Cut the following rectangles from coordinating print fabric: five 86" x 3" from length and thirty-six 11 ¼" x 3". Stitch one smaller rectangle to bottom edge of one block along one long edge. Stitch second long edge to top of second block (fig. C). Continue piecing blocks and rectangles in this manner until you have completed a strip of seven blocks and six rectangles, beginning and ending with a block. Complete a total of six strips

5. Stitch long edge of one 86" rectangle to long edge of one strip. Stitch second long edge to a second strip to join the two. Repeat to join all strips together, beginning and ending with strips (fig. D). Press seams to one side.

6. Cut blue fabric into two 39 ½" x 86" rectangles for quilt backing. Stitch together along one long edge; press seam open. Arrange layers as follows on flat surface. On bottom: backing, right side down; then batting, then pieced top, right side up. Baste all three

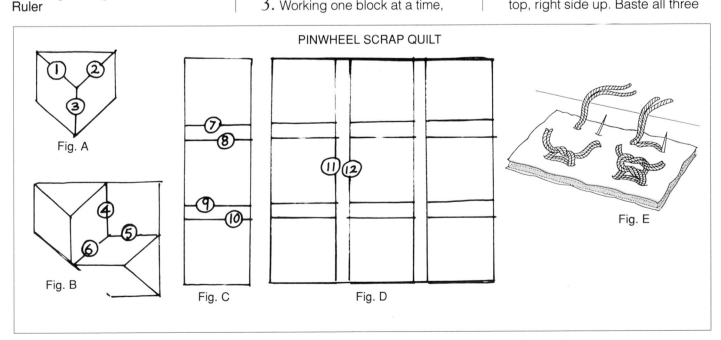

PINWHEEL SCRAP QUILT

Fig. A

Fig. B

Fig. C

Fig. D

Fig. E

together with broad basting stitch; mark center of each lengthwise and crosswise piecing strip with marking pencil.

7. Tuft layers together: Thread needle with four strands of embroidery floss. Starting on top, push needle straight through all three layers of quilt, leaving 4" tag end on top. Come up, go down again in same hole as first stitch and come up once more (see fig. E). Tie two tag ends together in square knot: right over left, left over right. Snip ends evenly to desired length; remove basting stitches.

8. To make binding, cut and piece a 10 yard x 4" strip from blue fabric. Back strip with batting. Pin long edge of binding strip to one edge of quilt on patchwork side. Stitch, ending ¼" from corner. Leave an overhang of 2" before cutting off strip. Continue until all four edges are bound.

9. Turn quilt patchwork side down; turn binding to back; turn raw edges under ½"; pin securely in place in as straight a line as possible; slipstitch in place, mitering corners.

STENCILED FLOWER QUILT

(Photo on p. 13)

Hot knife or X-acto knife
Heavyweight acetate
Cotton, cotton-blend muslin or broadcloth
Stretcher strips
Thumbtacks or staplegun
Blotting paper or paper towels
Masking tape
Acrylic fabric paint
Stenciling brush
Assorted calico scraps

STENCILED FLOWER QUILT

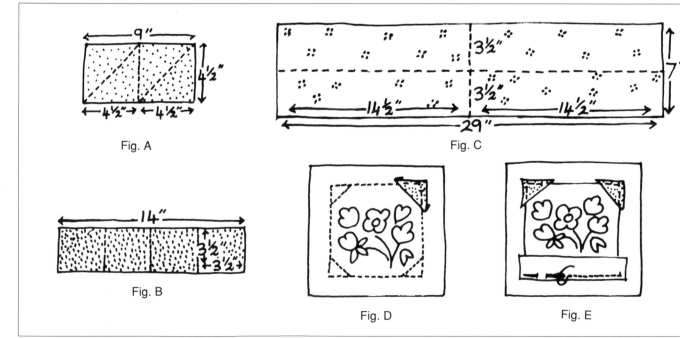

Fig. A

Fig. B

Fig. C

Fig. D

Fig. E

Batting
Quilting thread and needle
Quilt binding

1. Enlarge stenciling design to fill 14 ½" x 14 ½" squares (see p. 126). With hot knife or X-acto knife, cut out stencils. Stretch broadcloth on stretcher strips, securing with tacks or staplegun (see p. 126). With fabric side down, place flat on hard surface covered with blotting paper or paper towels. Center stencil on fabric. Cover nearby open areas of fabric with masking tape to keep them clean. Referring to photo or inventing your own color combination, paint stencil design on first square; repeat design for remaining squares; then stencil pillow sham (see p. 126 for stenciling tips).

2. To make borders for squares, cut calico fabric triangles (fig. A), corner squares (fig. B—make paper pattern) and strips (fig. C. Making a turnback and using blindstitch, sew diagonal of each triangle (fig. D). Pin other two sides of triangle and repeat all corners. With a running stitch, sew on calico border strips with fabric face down (fig. E). Flip border right side up and pin. Repeat on all sides. Apply corner squares; blindstitch seams.

3. Join bordered squares to form horizontal bands; join bands vertically to complete quilt; join outer borders. Baste batting and lining behind assembled quilt face. Using running stitch, quilt around all flower outlines with contrasting color thread; quilt border pattern with thread to match background (see p. 123 for quilting). Finish quilt with contrasting binding, doubled for strength.

SCRAP ART PILLOWS
(Photo on p. 12)

4 artist's stretcher strips, 18" long
Thumbtacks or staplegun
Batting, muslin, colored cotton and backing fabric, one 18" x 18" square of each per pillow
Brown paper
Scraps of gingham, calico and printed fabric in harmonious colors
Matching cotton sewing thread
Polyester fiberfill

Tricia   *Below are design diagrams for the three pillows pictured. Directions are given for the composition shown in the first diagram. Use the same technique to make the other two compositions or invent your own. If you begin with compatible colors, it's easy to establish design and color scheme as you go, laying pieces on top of the pillow base to find a pleasing arrangement.*

1. Stretch muslin on stretcher strips, tacking in place with thumbtacks or staplegun (see p. 126). Baste batting on top of muslin; lay colored cotton on top of batting.

2. Use brown paper to make pattern pieces: one right triangle with two 8" legs for corners, one wide center strip 15" x 4 ½" and one narrow center strip 15" x 2 ½".

3. Using paper pattern, cut out four fabric triangles; lay on top of pillow corners. Cut out one wide strip to run horizontally and one to run vertically across center of pillow (like a plus sign); cut two narrow strips to lay on top of each wide strip.

4. Remove all pieces and hand- or machine-stitch one by one on top of base fabric, sewing right through all layers. (Handstitching may be done in frame; to machine-stitch, first remove work from stretcher strips.) Position piece on pillow base with right sides together; sew ¼" seam along one edge of piece; flip over; baste down any raw edges that fall along pillow seam; turn remaining edges under ¼" and topstitch or edgestitch in place. Repeat with all pieces. Mount and stuff pillow (see p. 123).

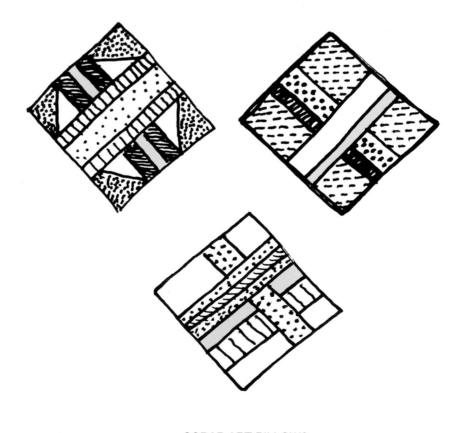

SCRAP ART PILLOWS

EMBROIDERED MONO-GRAMS AND BIRTHDAY FLOWERS
(Photo on p. 14)

Trace Erase ™ fabric or plain tissue paper
Article of your choice — towel, pillowslip, robe, placemat, etc.
Six-strand cotton embroidery floss, desired colors
Embroidery hoop and needle

1. Enlarge, then trace design onto Trace Erase™ fabric or tissue paper (see p. 126). Overlap and arrange initials and flowers to achieve the look you desire.

2. Stretch material to be embroidered in hoop and baste Trace Erase™ or tissue to fabric with design on top. Using three strands of embroidery floss and working through tissue and fabric together, embroider initials in rows of chain stitch (see p. 119), following direction of letter.

3. Using full six strands of floss, embroider flowers, leaves and stems, following stitch diagram. Using two strands of floss, embroider outlines of flowers; broken lines on charts indicate direction of stitches. When embroidery is complete, tear away Trace Erase™ or tissue.

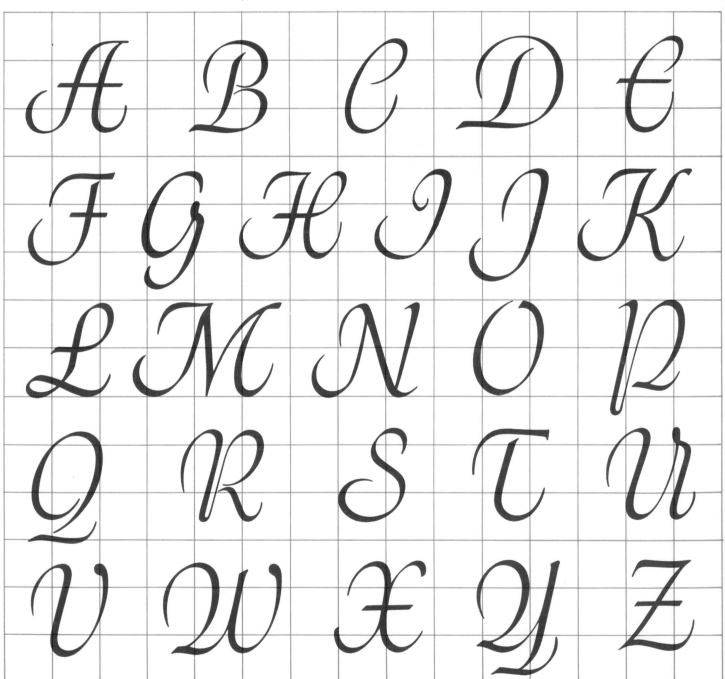

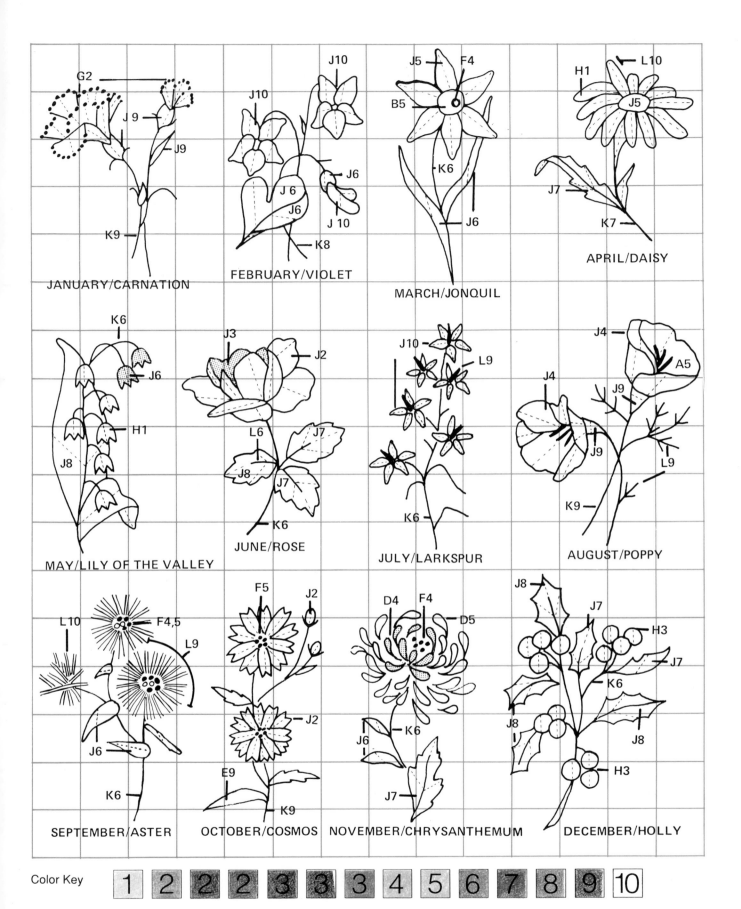

JANUARY/CARNATION
FEBRUARY/VIOLET
MARCH/JONQUIL
APRIL/DAISY

MAY/LILY OF THE VALLEY
JUNE/ROSE
JULY/LARKSPUR
AUGUST/POPPY

SEPTEMBER/ASTER
OCTOBER/COSMOS
NOVEMBER/CHRYSANTHEMUM
DECEMBER/HOLLY

Color Key   1 2 2 2 3 3 3 4 5 6 7 8 9 10

A. Bullion knots
B. Buttonhole stitch
C. Chain stitch

D. Detached chain stitch (Lazy daisy)
E. Fishbone stitch
F. French knots

G. French knots on long stitch
H. Padded satin stitch
J. Satin stitch

K. Stem stitch
L. Straight stitch

73

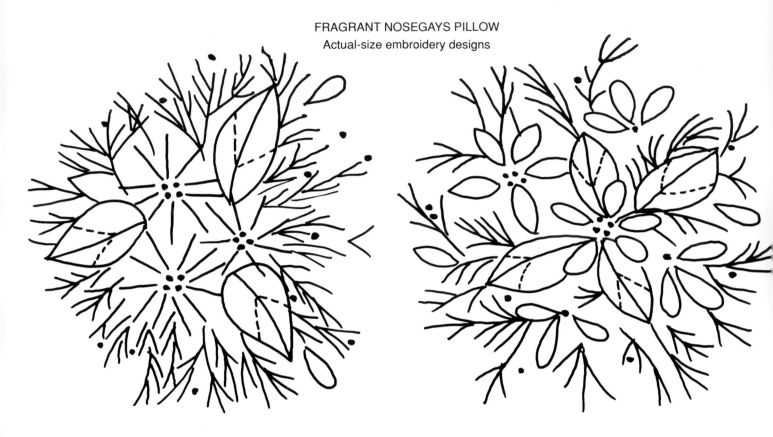

QUEEN ANNE'S FRAGRANT NOSEGAYS PILLOW
(Photo on p. 17)

Finished size: 10" x 10", plus ruffle

White fabric, ½ yard
Trace Erase™ pen or hard pencil
Dressmaker's carbon
4 artist's stretcher strips, 14" long
White pearl cotton, 1 skein
Six-strand ivory cotton embroidery floss, 1 skein
⅛"-wide Offray satin ribbon, 3 yards each white and ivory
⅜"-wide Offray satin ribbon, 2 yards ivory
No. 18 chenille needle
No. 9 crewel or beading needle
Small pearl beads, about 90
⅜"-wide scalloped ivory lace trim, 3 yards
1 ½"-wide white pre-gathered

eyelet trim, 1 ⅓ yards
Polyester fiberfill
Small inner pillow of potpourri or perfumed sachet

1. Cut two 11" squares from fabric; set one aside for backing and mount the other on stretcher frame (see p. 126). Using Trace Erase™ pen or hard pencil, divide fabric with horizontal and vertical center lines to form four equal boxes. Trace actual-size designs shown below. Alternating designs, use dressmaker's carbon to transfer one design in each box (see p. 126), centering and allowing for ½" seam allowances all around.

2. With two strands of ivory floss, first complete stem- and straight-stitch grasses (see p. 119). Next, using fishbone stitch, work leaves with two strands of white floss, keeping stitches just close enough to cover fabric.

3. Using ivory ribbon, straight stitch the flower petals in center of heart, keeping ribbon flat on surface of fabric; with same ribbon, stitch ivory lazy daisy petals in round design, taking extra care to control twisting of ribbon (see p. 124 for ribbon embroidery).

With white ribbon, stitch remaining lazy daisy blossoms in all squares.

4. Using single strand of ivory floss or matching sewing thread, attach simulated pearl beads in positions indicated by dots on design. Come up on one side of dot, thread floss through bead, go down on other side of dot. Remove embroidery from frame.

5. Cut two 11" lengths of ⅜"-wide ivory ribbon and four 11" lengths ivory lace. Baste lace along both long edges of each ribbon length; stitch to pillow front along horizontal and vertical center lines. Baste remaining ivory lace along one edge of remaining ivory ribbon; with lace facing towards pillow center, stitch to pillow front ½" from outer edge, carefully mitering corners.

6. With right sides facing, stitch eyelet along pillow front edges, allowing for extra fullness around corners. Leaving one edge open, stitch pillow front to back with right sides together and ½" seam allowances (see p. 123). Trim seams; turn to right side and insert fiberfill and perfumed small pillow. Slipstitch opening closed.

WILDFLOWER AND LACE PILLOW

(Photo on p. 17)

Finished size: 14" x 14"
14-mesh pink Aida cloth
4 artist's stretcher strips,18" long
Six-strand white cotton embroi-
    dery floss, ivory and white
White pearl cotton
No. 18 tapestry needle
No. 4 and no.18 crewel needles
Pillow backing fabric
Ruffled lace trim
Polyester fiberfill

1. Establish center of fabric by folding in half and half again. Mount fabric in stretcher strip frame (see p. 126). With white pearl cotton in no. 18 tapestry needle, follow chart and work cross-stitch octagonal border (see p. 119 for stitches). Enlarge embroidery design to fit inside octagonal cross-stitch border; transfer to fabric (see p. 126), centering design inside border.

2. With four strands of embroi-dery floss and no. 4 crewel nee-dle, embroider flowers. For carna-tion, work petals in raised stem stitch with ivory, for rose, work petals in buttonhole stitch with ivory, outer leaves in lazy daisy stitch with ivory, center in french knot with white and small leaves behind rose in fishbone stitch with ivory. For small daisies, work in lazy daisy stitch with french knot centers, using white; for but-terfly, work wings in satin stitch, body in a long bullion knot and antennae in french knots on long stitch, using white. For berries, work in padded satin stitch, using ivory; for large leaf, use laid work and tied split stitch in ivory; for tiny buds, work in french knots and stem stitch using both colors. All stems are worked in stem stitch, using either color.

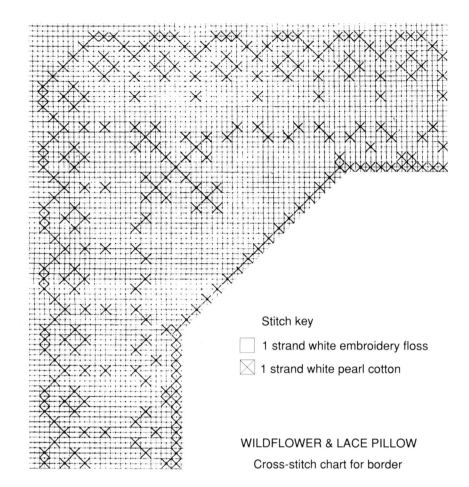

Stitch key

☐	1 strand white embroidery floss
☒	1 strand white pearl cotton

WILDFLOWER & LACE PILLOW

Cross-stitch chart for border

3. Using no. 18 tapestry needle, work outer cross-stitch border, following chart and using pearl cotton and single strand of floss to create lace effect. Trim, mount and stuff pillow (see p. 123).

Embroidery design

QUEEN ANNE'S BASKET OF RIBBON FLOWERS PILLOW

(Photo on p. 17)

Finished size: 11 ½" x 15 ½",
  plus ruffle
White fabric, ½ yard
Dressmaker's carbon
Embroidery hoop or frame
Six-strand cotton embroidery
  floss, white and ivory
Embroidery needle
⅛"-wide Offray satin ribbon:
  3 ½ yards ivory, 2 yards white
No. 18 chenille needle
1 ½"-wide white pre-gathered
  eyelet trim, 2 yards
White sewing thread
Polyester fiberfill or pillow form

1. Cut two 12 ½" x 16 ½" rectangles from fabric; set one aside for backing. Enlarge design; transfer design using dressmaker's carbon, centering on right side of pillow front (see p. 126).

2. Place fabric in embroidery hoop or frame (see p. 126). Using three strands of embroidery floss, work basket rim and handles in ivory with slanting satin stitch; fill in basket with ivory cross bars. Using chenille needle, work white ribbon french knots and ivory ribbon satin stitch for large flowers, keeping ribbon flat (see p. 124 for ribbon embroidery). For small flowers, using various combinations of white and ivory floss, three strands, embroider french knot centers and lazy daisy stitch petals and leaves; use four strands of white floss to stem stitch stems.

3. With right sides facing, stitch eyelet trim to edges of embroidered rectangle, using ½" seams and allowing extra fullness around corners. With right sides facing, stitch pillow front to back,

Embroidery design

using ½" seams and leaving an 8" opening along bottom edge. Trim seams, turn to right side. Fill firmly with fiberfill; slipstitch opening closed (see p. 123).

SMOCKED NIGHTDRESS

(Photo on p. 18)

Size: Since smocking is elastic,
  one size fits all in width. Adjust
  depth of smocking as needed
  to fit.
60"-wide white satin or silklike
  fabric, 3 ½ yards
Sewing thread, white and contrasting color
Smocking spot transfer or Trace
  Erase ™ grid

Six-strand cotton embroidery
  floss in desired colors
Embroidery needle
Straight pins with round, col-
  ored-glass heads

1. Cut two 55" x 60" rectangles from fabric (dress front and back; both will be smocked identically). Before smocking, finish upper edge of each piece with spit-and-roll hem: Take raw edges of fabric between thumb and forefinger; roll tightly several times; moisten your thumb to make fabric more pliable. Secure roll with whipstitch.

2. Transfer dots or baste Trace Erase™ grid to wrong side of fabric area to be smocked, starting 2" from one 60"-wide edge and continuing down for about 3 ½", leaving about ½" for seams along side edges (see p. 125 for smocking).

3. Thread needle with more than enough contrasting-color thread to complete a line of gathers; at right-hand edge, start with a knot

and a backstitch to secure thread firmly; following dots, run gathering threads through fabric. Come up through first dot, go down through next dot; repeat on each succeeding row to form "reeds" or vertical folds of identical size.

4. When all gathering threads are in place, lay fabric flat on table; pull up on threads in pairs until folds lie side by side. Secure gathers by twisting each pair of threads around a pin placed at edge of folds. Thread needle with two to four strands of floss, depending on delicacy of smocking desired.

5. The basic stitches used on the nightdresses pictured are cable stitch, diamond lattice stitch and chevron stitch. Follow stitch arrangement shown (fig. A) or create a stitch arrangement of your own.

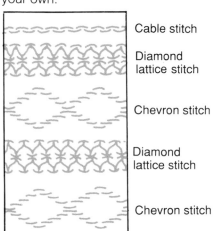

Cable stitch

Diamond lattice stitch

Chevron stitch

Diamond lattice stitch

Chevron stitch

Fig. A

6. When smocking is complete, set gathers by steaming them with steam iron; after steaming, stitches will stand out clearly and reeds will be beautifully rounded. When completely dry, remove gathering threads. Stitch smocked front to back along side edges, using french seams for a professional look and to avoid fraying; finish lower edge with spit-and-roll hem.

7. To make straps, cut four ½" x 16" strips from fabric. With right sides facing, fold in half lengthwise; stitch along long edge with ¼" seam; trim seam. To turn strap, thread blunt needle with double thread; secure to one end of strap; run needle and thread

SMOCKED NIGHTDRESS

through narrow tube of strap and pull to turn inside out (this is called a rouleau strap). Stitch two straps, side by side, to each shoulder edge on wrong side over smocking, taking care not to let stitches show on right side.

EMBROIDERED TAP PANTS
(Photo on p. 19)

Size: Directions and pattern given are for size medium (finished waist measurement 28")
Tracing paper or tissue
45"-wide peach silk crepe de chine or peau de soie, or similar fabric, 1 yard
Sewing thread, peach and ivory
Trace Erase™ pen
Fine cotton batiste, ½ yard
Embroidery hoop and needle
Six-strand cotton embroidery floss in Ivory and light peach (slightly paler than fabric)
¼"-wide ivory scalloped lace trim, 2 ½ yards
One small button

1. Enlarge pattern on tracing or tissue paper (see p. 126); cut out. Outline pattern pieces on fabric with basting stitches: Outline two identical patterns first, placing arrow in same direction on straight grain of fabric, then flip pattern over, exactly reversing it, and outline two more pieces. Outline one 34" x 1" strip for waistband.

2. Transfer embroidery pattern to fabric using light-box method and Trace Erase™ pen . Refer to photo for placement of motifs, or make your own arrangement. On tap pants pictured, embroidery motifs are worked on lower left of front section; leaves are worked across bottom, edge of left front and rightmost corner of right front.

3. Stretch a square of batiste tightly in embroidery hoop, preferably on a stand (see p. 126), then baste design area of pants fabric on top (this avoids stretching bias fabric in frame). With two strands of floss, work design, embroidering through silk fabric and batiste. Work padded satin stitch on all larger areas, work all small circles with french knots, peacock's feathers with buttonhole stitch circles, peacock's feet with bullion knots, stems with whipped chain stitch and leaves in lazy daisy stitch (see p. 119). After stitching, cut away unwanted batiste close against stitching on reverse side.

4. Right sides facing, baste front sections together along curved edge between dots; repeat with back sections. Press open seams and work point turc or punch stitch over joins (see p.125). Stitch front to back along side seams using french seam. Leave 2 ½" unstitched on upper portion of left side; narrow-hem this section to clean-finish for an opening. Stitch pants together along inside leg, using french seam.

5. Stitch waistband fabric to upper edge of pants, extending ½" over each narrow-hemmed area; stitch overlap even with side seams; turn waistband to back, then slipstitch in place, turning raw edge under ¼". Make a buttonhole loop from peach floss on

front left top; stitch button on back left top to correspond. Handstitch lace to lower edges with point de Paris or pin stitch Cut two 7" lengths of lace: Place center of each length on each side seam 1 ¼" from bottom edge; angle so ends of lace meet lace on lower edge; stitch in place.

LINGERIE BAG
(Photo on p. 19)

Finished size: 15 ½" x 20"
45"-wide white organdy fabric, ¾ yard
Six-strand cotton embroidery floss, light blue
Embroidery needle
⅛"-wide white double-faced satin ribbon, 1 yard
1"-wide Offray white double-faced satin ribbon, 1 ½ yards
1"-wide Offray ivory double-faced satin ribbon, 2 yards
Two small round white or clear buttons
⅜"-wide white grosgrain ribbon, 1 yard

1. Cut fabric into a 20" x 42" rectangle. Press all edges under ⅛", then ⅛" again. Using three strands of floss, work buttonhole

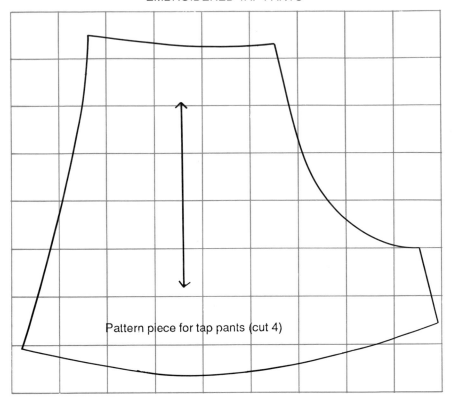

Pattern piece for tap pants (cut 4)

stitch (see p. 119) along the two short edges, ⅛" in length over pressed edge to finish. With wrong sides facing, fold rectangle 15 ½" from one short edge to make bag. The remaining 11" will be folded over later to form bag flap. Work buttonhole stitch along the two long edges in same manner on both bag base and bag flap to secure. Fold flap over to front; measure in 4" from each side edge and mark points on flap and bag base front.

2. Cut two circles 2" in diameter from remaining fabric; place button in center of each; stitch close to edges, then gather together. Trim away any excess fabric, then

stitch covered buttons to marked points on bag base front. Using blue floss, make chain-stitch buttonloops on flap opposite.

3. Following directions for ribbon roses (see p. 124), make three white and four ivory roses from 1"-wide satin ribbon. Loop grosgrain ribbon in all directions to make starburst shape approximately 4 ½" in diameter; stitch together at center. Cut ⅛"-wide white satin ribbon into 8" lengths; press along a scissor or straightedge to make curls. Stitch uncurled edge of each to starburst center, then stitch ribbon roses over center. Sew entire ribbon arrangement to center bottom of bag flap.

Actual–size embroidery design

CODE FLAG BELT
(Photo on p. 20)

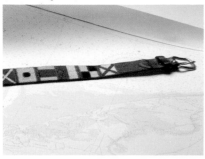

12-mesh needlepoint canvas
Acrylic paint (optional)
Paintbrush
Persian wool in red, blue, yellow,
  white, black and dark green or
  desired background color
Tapestry needle

Erica This belt is best professionally mounted, so be very accurate about sizes and measurements before you begin. Take his waist measurement. For a belt finished in leather, the measurement should go from the end of the buckle to the first hole. Make sure the belt, when finished, will not be too wide to fit through his belt loops. The belt pictured has a dark green background; heraldic colors of code flags are best set off by very light or very dark grounds such as navy, black, burgundy, white cream or pastel green. If you choose a dark background color, paint your canvas with acrylic paint of the same color before beginning to stitch so that no white will appear at edges when they are turned back to mount the belt.

1. Count out your design on graph paper, following alphabet charts given, allowing 12 squares for every letter and at least 2 squares between letters. Find center of complete design and match it to center of canvas. Check size of finished design on canvas, and before you begin to stitch, adjust length of design to fit finished belt length by adding or removing space between letters and at either end.

2. Working in tent stitch (continental stitch), fill in letters first (see p. 122). Next, using background color, fill in space between letters and work at least two rows across top and bottom edges of lettering. Block and mount needlepoint (see p. 119).

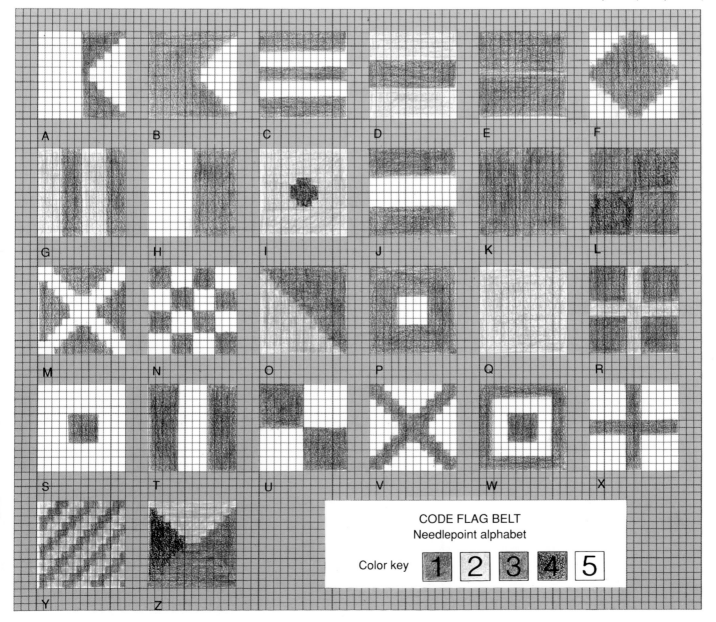

CODE FLAG BELT
Needlepoint alphabet

Color key   1   2   3   4   5

NEEDLEPOINT SLIPPERS
(Photo on p. 20)

Shaped slipper pattern for uppers
   from shoemaker in correct size
14-mesh needlepoint canvas
Permanent marker
Blunt tapestry needle
Needlepoint yarn in desired colors

Trica Before you start, locate a shoemaker who will mount your needlepoint slippers professionally, perhaps through a local needlepoint store. The shoemaker will provide a shaped cardboard pattern for the uppers, which you can then outline on your canvas. To personalize the design, you could trace initials in the center of the upper and work in two colors as in the slippers pictured; you could use a code flag initial in bright nautical colors or you might like to try plaid point to make a pair of tartan slippers (a good use for leftover yarns).

1. Lay canvas over cardboard pattern for slipper upper, making sure canvas threads are lined up running straight down center of foot. Outline pattern shape with permanent marker, then flip pattern over and outline it on canvas in reverse so that you have one left and one right foot (leave a couple inches of space between the two patterns for mounting).

2. Trace the pattern outline on paper and work out your needlepoint design (see monograms on p. 72, code flag alphabet on p. 79 and plaid point directions on p. 122).

3. Transfer design to canvas (see p. 126); fill in design using tent stitch (continental stitch—see p.

122). Wash and block work if necessary; have slippers finished professionally.

TIE CASE
(Photo on p. 21)

Finished size: 16 ½" x 4 ¼"
Polyester batting, 16 ½" x 9"
   rectangle
Heavyweight cardboard, 15 ¾" x
   3 ¾" rectangle
Fabric glue
Moire fabric, ½ yard each black
   and burgundy
Matching sewing thread
Two shank buttons ¾" diameter

Trica This elegant tie case in black moire has a stiffened center section with two flaps on either side. Flaps fold over ties and are closed with loops; fabric-covered buttons in burgundy moire match the lining.

1. Cut batting in half lengthwise; glue one section each to front and back of cardboard rectangle. Referring to diagram below and adding ½" all around, cut out the following: in black, one complete piece (indicated by solid outline);

in burgundy, one of each section (indicated by broken lines); also in burgundy, two rectangles each ¾" x 4 ½" (tie bar holders) and ¾" x 2 ½" (buttonloops).

2. With right sides together, fold each tie bar holder rectangle in half lengthwise; stitch close to raw edge using ¼" seam. Trim seam and turn to right side. Place one completed tie bar holder across width of center burgundy section 2 ½" from top; place second tie bar holder 2 ½" from bottom edge; baste in place along side edges. Assemble buttonloop rectangles in same manner as tie bar holders. Fold each in half widthwise to form a loop; baste raw edges of each to edge of burgundy fabric indicated by star on diagram.

3. With right sides together, stitch burgundy sections together along long edges to form one complete section. With right sides together, stitch front to back using ½" seams and leaving bottom of center section unstitched. Turn to right side; press, insert cardboard along center section; slipstitch opening closed.

4. From remaining burgundy fabric, cut two circles 1 ½" in diameter. Stitch a row of gathering stitches close to edge. Place button in center of wrong side of circle; draw gathers together and secure. Stitch button in place to correspond with buttonloop placement.

Tie case diagram

7 ¾"
4 ¾"
3"
3 ¾"
2 ¾"
16 ½"

9 ½" Actual-size tie case loop

Actual-size tie case holder

HIS AND HER SWEATERS

(Photo on p. 22)

Finished chest/bust size: 46"
Pingouin Superwash sportweight yarn or any yarn to obtain specified gauge, 1 ¾ oz (50 g) skeins, 10 skeins MC, 2 skeins of each of 4 CC
Knitting needles, one pair each size 4 and size 3 or size to obtain correct gauge
16" circular knitting needle, size 3
GAUGE: 30 stitches and 36 rows = 4" (10 cm) in St st using larger needles. To save time, take time to check gauge.

ABBREVIATIONS USED:
beg = beginning
CC = contrasting color
Dec = decrease
Inc = increase
k = knit
MC = main color
pat = pattern
p = purl
RS = right side
rep = repeat
sl = slip
st = stitch
St st = Stockinette stitch
WS = wrong side

STITCHES USED:
K1, p1 rib: *K1, p1; rep from * across. On all following rows, k the k sts and p the p sts as they face you.
St st: K 1 row, p 1 row.
Sl 1: Holding yarn at wrong side of knitting, pass st purlwise from left to right needle without working.
Selvedge stitch: Sl 1 at beg and end of each RS row to make firm edge.
Jacquard pat: Work in St st with MC; follow RS rows of chart from right to left and WS rows from left to right, overlapping yarns on WS when you change colors.
See page 122 for knitting basics.

Erica *Because threads left lying across the wrong side will catch if carried too far from one point to another, yarn is overlappped every few stitches, as shown in figs. A–D. Sport weight yarn gives a very dense fabric; for a lighter sweater, you may substitute fingering weight. Knit a practice swatch first to test your gauge and pattern.*

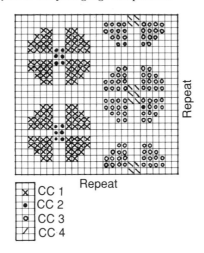

	CC 1
×	CC 1
•	CC 2
⊚	CC 3
╱	CC 4

Repeat

1. Back: Using smaller needles and MC, cast on 172 sts. Work in k1, p1 rib for 3", end RS. Change to larger needles; p 1 row. Beg St st and jacquard pat as follows: Row 1(RS) Sl 1 (selvedge st), k 1, work 24 st rep of chart 7 times, work first st of chart, sl 1 (selvedge st). Rep 24 rows of jacquard pat until 24" or desired length from beg; bind off.

2. Front: Work same as back until 3" (about 27 rows) shorter than

back. Shape neck: K 52 in pat, join 2nd ball of MC; bind off center 68 stitches for front neck, k52 in pat. Working both sides at same time with separate balls of yarn, continue pat, dec 1 st each neck edge each row 5 times—47 sts each side. Work even until same length as back, matching pat; bind off.

3. Sleeves: Using smaller needles and MC, cast on 60 sts. Work in k 1, p 1 rib for 2", end RS. Change to larger needles; p 1 row, increasing 12 sts evenly spaced across—72 sts. Beg St st and jacquard pat as follows: Row 1 (RS): Sl 1 (selvedge st); follow chart, starting first rep at 17th st, work entire 24 st rep twice, k first 10 sts of chart, sl 1 (selvedge st). Maintain jacquard pat, inc 1 st each end every 5th row 26 times—126 sts. Work even until 17" from beg or desired length; bind off.

4. Finishing: Block pieces: Pin face down to padded surface with rust-proof pins, referring to measurement diagram; steam lightly with steam iron (do not rest weight of iron on fabric; do not block ribbed borders). Let dry completely. Sew shoulder seams. Mark side edge 8 ½" from shoulder seam for underarm; sew sleeve top to straight edge of armhole, centering between markers. Sew side, sleeve seams.

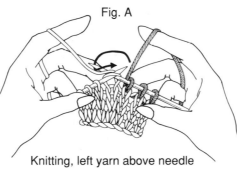

Fig. A

Knitting, left yarn above needle

Fig. B

Knitting, left yarn below needle

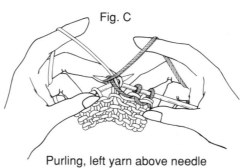

Fig. C

Purling, left yarn above needle

Fig. D

Purling, left yarn below needle

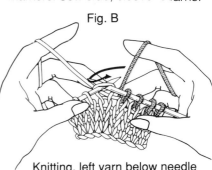

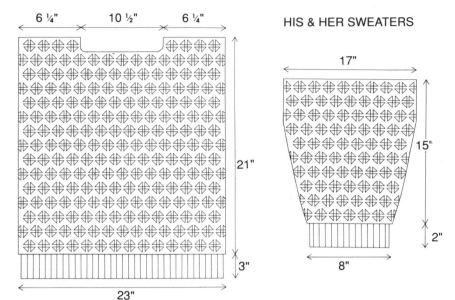

HIS & HER SWEATERS

6 ¼" 10 ½" 6 ¼"

23"

21"

3"

17"

15"

2"

8"

STENCILED SWEATSHIRTS

Stenciling designs

5. Collar: Mark center front neck. WS facing, using circular needle and MC, pick up 150 sts evenly spaced around neck edge, beg and end at center front. Do not join work; collar is divided at center front. Row 1 (RS): Sl 1 (selvedge st), work k1,p1 ribbing to last st, sl 1 (selvedge st). Ros 2:the k sts and p the p sts as they face you. Rep rows 1 and 2 until collar measures 7". Bind off all sts loosely in ribbing.

STENCILED SWEAT-SHIRTS
(Photo on p. 23)

Heavy acetate
X -acto knife or hot knife
Masking tape
Stencil brush
Illinois Bronze acrylic fabric paint
2 sheets cardboard
Work table, paper towels, water
Purchased sweatshirt

1. Enlarge and draw designs on paper in full scale (see p. 126), arranging to cover sweatshirt front. Arrange motifs in horizontal rows. Cover worktable with heavy cardboard. Tape drawing to back of acetate. Using X-acto or hot knife, cut out stencils.

2. Lay sweatshirt out on work-table right side up. Slide a piece of cardboard between back and front of shirt so paint will not penetrate to reverse side. Using one color at a time, stencil on designs (see p. 126).

Trica Paint dries immediately, but before washing, allow the paint to cure for two or three days. To wash, turn inside out and wash in cool water, lay out on towel to dry. Paint is permanent and should not fade provided these directions are followed.

PADDED SATIN HANGER

(Photo on p. 24)

⅛"–1"-wide ribbons, double-faced and single-faced satin and picot-edged, in desired colors
Matching sewing thread
Purchased white satin padded hanger (optional)
Wooden dress hanger (optional)
45"-wide white satin, 1 yard (optional)
Batting, two 6" x 10" pieces (optional)

Erica *Cover a wooden hanger from scratch, or purchase a padded hanger and simply add roses and bows.*

1. For purchased hanger, make assorted ribbon roses (see p. 124); sew individually to center area of hanger in a cluster or bouquet. Make assorted ribbon bows; tack around roses as desired.

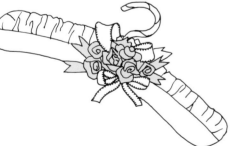

2. To cover a wooden hanger, proceed as follows. From satin, cut two 3 ½" x 20" pieces, two 3 ½" x 10" pieces and one 1 ½" x 10" bias strip. Fold bias strip in half lengthwise; stitch ¼" from folded edge and trim seam allowance to ½". Turn right side out to make a tube. Slip tube over hook of hanger: Do not cut off excess at this time.

3. Wrap batting around each arm of hanger; baste raw edge in place, joining ends at center. Hand- or machine-gather both edges of 20" fabric pieces; pull up gathers to 10". With right sides together, pin and stitch one edge of each gathered piece to one edge of each 10" piece. Turn free edge of 10" pieces ½" to wrong side; press. With gathers on top, wrap and pin a piece around one arm of hanger. By hand, neatly and securely slipstitch folded edge to gathered edge. Repeat for second arm of hanger, joining pieces at center and securing end of bias tubing.

4. Tie knot in bias tubing at end of hook; cut off excess. Turn in and sew fabric at ends of hanger. Wrap a length of 1"-wide ribbon around center join; tie ends in a bow at back. Make and sew on roses and bows as in step 1.

RING BEARER'S PILLOW

(Photo on p. 24)

Finished size: 10" x 10", plus 3" ruffle
45"-wide white moire fabric, ⅜ yard
White satin, 6" x 12" piece
Matching sewing thread
Trace Erase™ pen
Embroidery needle and hoop
Six-strand cotton embroidery floss, few feet turquoise or desired color
Batting, ⅜ yard
Muslin, 11" x 11" piece
Offray satin ribbons:
　⅛"-wide double-faced, ⅝ yard white, 1 ⅝ yards turquoise
　¼"-wide double-faced, 3 yards white
　2 ¼"-wide single-faced, ⅝ yard white

Variety of ¼"–⅝"-wide, double- and single-faced, plain and picot-edged, white, turquoise and jade or desired colors
2 "gold" rings (available at party supply stores)
3"-wide pre-gathered lace, 1 ¼ yards white
10" zipper, white
Polyester fiberfill or pillow form

1. Enlarge heart pattern (see p. 126). From moire, cut one 11" x 11" front and two 64" x 11" backs. From satin, cut two hearts; from batting, cut one 11" x 11" front and one heart. With fine pen, carefully write names of bride and groom and wedding date on right side of one satin heart. With two strands of floss, embroider names and date in backstitch, following pen markings.

2. Baste batting to wrong side of embroidered heart. Right sides together, using ½" seam allowance, stitch hearts together; trim batting in seam allowance; clip and trim seam allowance at point and curves. Carefully make 3" slash on heart back; carefully turn heart right side out through slash, slipstitch opening and press. Baste batting, then muslin to wrong side of moire front. Center and slipstitch embroidered heart to pillow front.

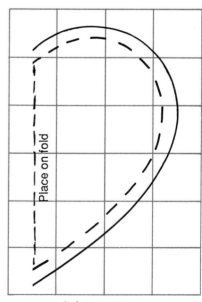

½ heart pattern

3. Using various ribbons, make ribbon roses as desired (see p.

124). Make one bow each from white and turquoise ⅛"-wide ribbons. Starting at pillow front upper left corner, pin roses in a cascading arrangement to top left side of heart, then from bottom right side of heart to lower right of pillow front. Arrange and pin bows and a few small roses to top left side of heart as desired; securely stitch to pillow front. Tie "gold" rings in place.

4. With right sides together and raw edges matching, baste lace around pillow front. Press under ¾" on one long edge of each moire back piece. Stitch one pressed edge along zipper. Trim back to 11" x 11". Cut two 14"-wide ribbons in half crosswise; overlap long edges ⅛" and zigzag stitch together to make one 44" x 11" piece; baste over zipper to back at raw edges (this will enable ring bearer to hold pillow securely). With right sides together, using ½" seam allowance, stitch pillow front to back leaving zipper open.

5. Trim batting in seam allowance; clip corners and turn right side out through zipper opening. Insert fiberfill or pillow form and close zipper. Make four bows of ⅛"-wide turquoise ribbon and four bows of ¼"-wide white ribbon; securely stitch each turquoise bow to center of each white bow; join each bow to corner of pillow.

RIBBON & LACE GARTER
(Photo on p. 24)

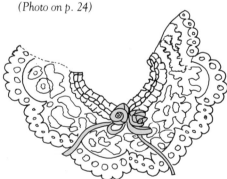

3"-wide pre-gathered white lace, ¾ yard
Matching sewing thread
Wright's ½"-wide white single-fold bias tape, ¾ yard
4"-wide elastic cut to measurement of thigh plus 1"

Small safety pin or yarn needle
⅛"-wide Offray satin ribbon, 20" turquoise and 10" white
Coordinating ribbons to make two ribbon roses

1. With right sides together, stitch raw ends of lace together. Using matching thread, zigzag stitch turquoise ribbon over gathered top edge of lace. With wrong sides together, topstitch edges of bias tape to top edge of lace to form casing, folding ends of bias tape under ¼".

2. Catch end of elastic in safety pin or yarn needle, pull elastic through casing; securely stitch ends together. Slipstitch open ends of casing. Make two ribbon roses (see p. 124) in desired colors and a white ribbon bow; securely tack bow and ribbon roses to front top edge of garter.

PRAYER BOOK COVER
(Photo on p. 26)

Brown paper
Trace Erase™ pen (optional)
Cotton, silk or satin fabric sufficient to cover book and make two 2" inside cover flaps
Poly-cotton lining, equivalent amount to fabric
Polyester felt, equivalent amount to fabric
Embroidery hoop
Six-strand cotton embroidery floss, 1 skein ivory
Pearl cotton embroidery floss, 1 skein white
⅛"-wide Offray ivory satin ribbon, ⅝ yard
¼"-wide Offray white satin ribbon, 3 yards
Tiny simulated pearl beads, about 30
No. 20 chenille needle for ribbon
No. 8 and 10 crewel needles

1. Measure overall size of book with tape measure: height, front-to-back measurement around

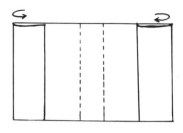

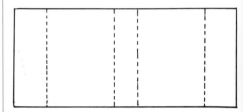

PRAYER BOOK COVER

spine taken with book closed (plus 2" at either side for flaps). Draw and cut out paper pattern to size. On straight grain of fabric, mark outlines of paper pattern with Trace Erase™ pen or basting stitches. Mark ½" all around for turnbacks.

2. Before cutting, trace actual-size embroidery design and transfer to fabric for front area of book (see p. 126). Mount fabric into embroidery hoop (see p. 126). With two strands of ivory floss, embroider grasses in stem stitch and straight stitch. With two strands of white floss, embroider leaves in fishbone stitch, keeping stitches just close enough to cover fabric (see p. 119 for stitches). With ivory ribbon and chenille needle, straight stitch flower petals, keeping ribbon flat on fabric (see p. 123 for ribbon embroidery). With white ribbon, stitch lazy daisy blossoms, taking care to control twist of ribbon.

3. Using one strand of ivory floss or matching sewing thread, join simulated pearl beads as indicated by dots on design chart. Come up on one side of dot; thread floss through bead; go down on other side of dot. Cut out fabric.

4. Cut 2 ¼" off either side of paper pattern and use it to cut felt to size of book without flaps. Cut lining same size as embroidered piece (book size including flaps and turnbacks). Center felt over lining with lining extending 2 ¼"

beyond each end of felt. Baste layers together. Turn lining with felt side face down on table; place embroidered fabric face down on lining. Machine-stitch ¼" in from raw edge all around, leaving a 6" opening at one side for turning. Trim and press turnbacks. Turn right side out and slipstitch opening closed.

5. Measure 2" in from each end of cover and machine-stitch straight down at either side to secure felt, stitching through all layers (fig. A). Using stitching lines as fold lines, press, fold down and slipstitch upper and lower edges together at top and bottom along folds (fig. B). Slip book inside, enclosing in flap at either side.

BOOKMARK
(Photo on p. 26)

Offray satin ribbons:
  1"-wide pink, 1 yard
  ⅜"-wide ivory, ½ yard
  ¼"-wide gold-edged white or peach, 1 yard
  1⁄16"-wide ivory, 1 yard
  1"-wide green, scrap
  ⅜"-wide picot-edged biscuit

ribbon, scrap
2 pearl beads, ½" diameter
Flat ivory button, 1" diameter with two center holes
Nylon invisible thread and sewing needle
Florist's leaves

1. Make ribbon rose, using ¼"-wide gold-edged ribbon (see p. 124). Cut 1⁄16"-wide ivory ribbon in half; thread one length partway through each hole of flat ivory button; knot firmly below button; knot two ends together; slide a pearl bead onto each free end; knot beads in place.

BOOKMARK

2. Fold 1"-wide pink ribbon in three tiered sections. Center doubled biscuit ribbon on top of pink ribbon tier; make bow of ⅜"-wide ivory ribbon and place on top of biscuit ribbon; place florist's leaves on top of bow for base of ribbon rose; place ribbon rose on top (see figs. A & B). Sew all layers firmly together; sew and glue base of folded pink ribbon to flat ivory button.

PRAYER BOOK COVER

Actual–size embroidery design

HAIRCLIP
(Photo on p. 26)

Offray satin ribbons:
  ¼"-wide white, 1 yard
  ¹⁄₁₆"-wide yellow, 3 yards
  ¼"-wide pink, 2 yards
  ¾"-wide white, 1 yard
Metal hairclip
Nylon invisible thread and sewing
  needle

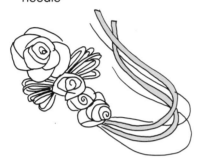

1. Using ¼"-wide ribbons, make
one large white ribbon rose and
three smaller pink ribbon roses
(see p 124). Cover hairclip with
white ribbon by winding over and
over. Sew ends of ribbon securely. Join bows and streamers of
yellow ribbon to clip; join ribbon
roses, stitching with nylon invisible thread.

BRIDE'S HANKY/CHRIS-
TENING BONNET
(Photo on p. 27)

Batiste, lawn or fine handkerchief
  linen, ¼ yard
Edging lace, 1 yard
Six-strand white cotton or pure
  silk embroidery floss
Embroidery hoop and needles
Silk ribbons for bonnet
Matching sewing thread

1. Before cutting hanky, embroider one corner, using design for
tap pants (see p.77), or any delicate stitching design you like. Cut
10½" x 10½" square from fabric;
join edging lace with punch or pin
stitch (see p. 125).

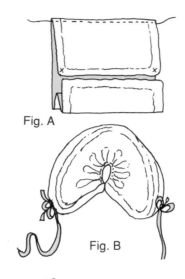

Fig. A

Fig. B

Erica *Alternatively, surround a
smaller square of fabric with a wider
portion of lace and apply tiny pearl
beads to the lace, using the method for
the beaded lace gown (p. 97).*

2. To convert hanky into bonnet,
lay hanky flat; fold two outer
edges to meet in center; press
lightly. Tack down lace corners of
one flap; unfold other flap and
refold slightly beyond crease;
pleat as shown; press (fig. A).

3. Run a gathering thread along
fold of unpleated flap; draw up
gathering so that a small open
circle forms at center back; fasten the two edges of lace together (fig. B). Place bows or ribbon
roses at front edges of bonnet;
join ribbon ties.

EMBROIDERED
ORGANDY TABLECLOTH
(Photo on p. 28)

Finished size: 36" x 36"
45"-wide white organdy, 1 ½
  yards
Shelf paper or tracing paper
Fine black permanent marker
Trace Erase™ pen or hard pencil
Embroidery hoop or frame
Six-strand cotton embroidery
  floss, 1 skein each medium
  orange, moss green, white and
  shocking pink
Silver metallic embroidery thread
  (such as DMC Fil d'Argent)
No. 9 embroidery needle
No. 20 chenille needle
White sewing thread
Graph paper

1. Cut 44" x 44" square from fabric; establish center by folding in
half and half again. Cut same
size pattern from shelf paper or
tracing paper; establish center
same way. Using permanent
marker, enlarge and trace
embroidery design onto paper
pattern (see p. 126): alternating

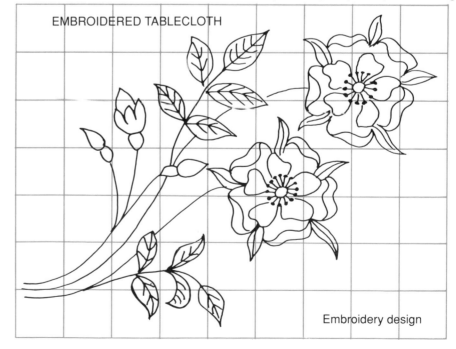

EMBROIDERED TABLECLOTH

Embroidery design

single and double flower motifs around center in a circle approximately 6" from center point; in each corner, place one flower motif running diagonally in from corner point (fold pattern to establish true diagonal).

2. When design is thoroughly dry, place organdy on top of paper pattern, lining up center crease marks; tape fabric down. Using hard pencil or Trace Erase™ pen, trace design onto fabric. Stretch fabric wrong side up in embroidery hoop or frame.

3. Using three strands of embroidery floss and referring to color photo, shadow stitch flowers, leaves and buds by working herringbone stitch from wrong side (see p. 119 for stitches). When all shadow work is complete, remount fabric in frame right side up and embroider details with silver metallic thread: flower centers in padded satin stitch, surrounded by french knots on long stitch and stems and leaf veins in stem stitch. When embroidery is complete, dampen and press face down into a thick towel or blanket. Press hem up on right side: Turn over 2" all around; press. Turn over another 2"; press.

Making pattern for mitered corners

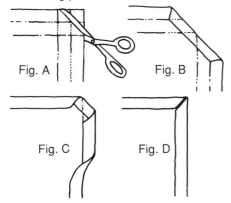

Fig. A   Fig. B

Fig. C   Fig. D

4. Make paper pattern for mitering corners: Using a sheet of graph paper, turn over and crease 2" along one edge; turn over and crease 2" again; repeat on one adjacent edge (fig. A). Open up and you will have four creased squares in the corner. Fold over diagonally ¼" above inmost corner point; cut along diagonal crease line (fig. B). Fold

cut edge ¼" over exactly at inmost corner point (fig. C). Refold straight edges along crease lines (fig. D); diagonal creases should butt to form a perfect mitered corner. Unfold; use pattern for each corner of cloth; slipstitch mitered corners of cloth with tiny invisible stitches. Baste hem; secure with white floss in point de Paris (p. 125)

Erica Alternatively, make and join a separate hem, using contrasting organdy and stitching with point de Paris in a deeper shade.

ALMOND ROSE FAVOR
(Photo on p. 29)

To make one favor:
 White nylon tulle, 5" x 5" square
 3 white Jordan Almonds
 2 ⅝"-wide fused-edge white or pink florist's ribbon, 30"
 Green florist's tape
 2 large florist's rose leaves
 White florist's stamens
 Green florist's wire, 9"
 Heavy thread

Erica Jordan Almonds are available at candy stores; floral items and wire are available in florist supply stores.

1. Trim tulle to form a circle about 5" in diameter. Place three Jordan Almonds in center; gather tulle around almonds with your fingers to form rose center. Double over the top inch of green florist's wire and push it inside gathered tulle among almonds to form rose stem. Holding three double stamens at base of gathered tulle, wrap tightly with white thread, securing almonds, gathered tulle and wire; bend stamens up around almonds. Trim tulle frill at base if necessary.

ALMOND ROSE FAVOR

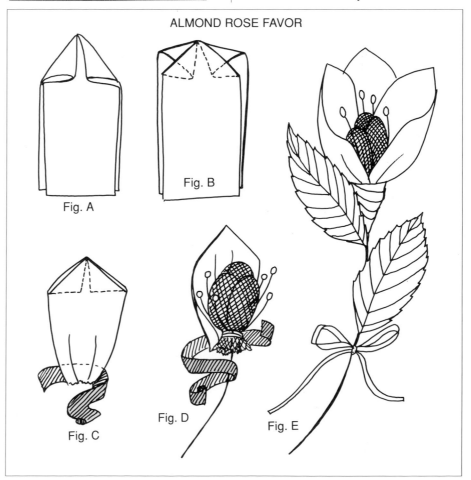

Fig. A   Fig. B

Fig. C   Fig. D   Fig. E

2. To form petals, cut three 9 ½" lengths of florist's ribbon. Fold each in half and press, right sides together, to measure 4 ¾". At fold, turn down; press corners to meet in center, forming arrow shape (fig. B). Open; turn right side out; where crease marks delineate triangles, push to inside and press (fig. C). Now petal has arrow-shaped top with right side out and no visible turnbacks.

3. With fingers, fold three pleats at base of first petal; using floral tape, secure petal around wire at base of almond cluster (figs. C & D). Tape next petal beside it, slightly overlapping; tape third petal to overlap second, surrounding rose center. Continue wrapping tape down wire, binding in two rose leaves as you go; complete by tying a small bow of ⅛"-wide ribbon to stem (fig. E).

LACE HEART RICE FAVOR BASKET
(Photo on p. 29)

Finished size: 3" x 4" basket with 2" handle
Tracing paper
White lace, 4" x 8" scrap
White glue
Cotton sewing thread, red and white
½"-wide pre-gathered lace ruffle, 1 yard
⅛"-wide satin ribbon, 12" each red and white
Red nylon tulle, 10" x 10" square
Rice or birdseed

1. Trace actual-size heart basket pattern onto paper and cut from lace. Stitch or glue gathered lace around top edges of lace basket. Right sides together, stitch extensions together along stitching line; turn basket right side out. Cut two 6" lengths from gathered lace; stitch or glue together along straight edge to form a two-sided

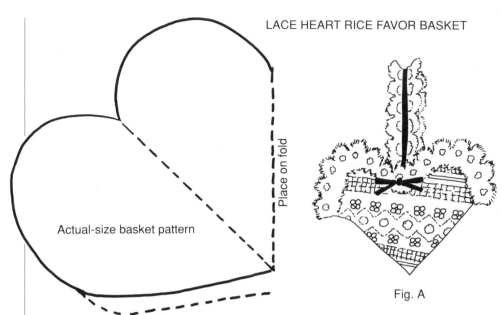

Actual-size basket pattern

Place on fold

Fig. A

ruffle for handle. Glue 6" length of red ribbon over center of ruffle to form handle; stitch each handle end to inside top center of heart on each side of basket (see fig. A). Make two small bows with remaining red ribbon; stitch or glue to sides of basket at handle base (see fig. A). Place rice in center of tulle square; gather ends and tie with white ribbon.

Erica *After the wedding, fill basket with potpourri, candy, soaps, miniature pinecones, etc., to hang on Christmas tree, in a bathroom, bedroom or closet.*

LACE SACK FILLED WITH RICE OR HEART SOAP
(Photo on p. 29)

2 ½"-wide lace, 6" length
Nylon tulle, 2 ½" x 6", or 2 ½"-wide Offray pink or purple satin ribbon, 6" length
⅛"-wide Offray purple, pink or off-white satin ribbon, 8" length
Off-white sewing thread
Pinking shears

Small amount of rice or birdseed, or one small heart-shaped soap for each sack

1. Cut short ends of tulle and raw ends of lace with pinking shears. Pin tulle to wrong side of lace. Tulle side in, fold in half crosswise and stitch along three sides ¼" in from edges to form sack, leaving one short end open. Turn right side out; fill with rice, birdseed or soap; tie with ribbon.

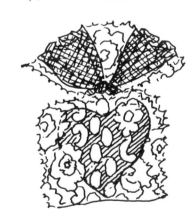

FLOWER GIRL'S SMOCKED DRESS

(Photo on p. 30)

Size: Small (2T–4T), large (4–6)
Layout paper or shelf paper
48"-wide cotton print or plain fabric, 2 yards
Iron-on smocking spot transfer or Trace Erase™ smocking grid
Matching sewing or quilting thread of strong cotton
Six-strand cotton embroidery floss in desired colors
⅞"-wide grosgrain ribbon, 4 yards
1 ½"-wide white eyelet lace, 2 yards
2 o 3 small buttons

Erica Back and front are cut as rectangles and after smocking, are shaped to form bodice. Shaping of armholes and shoulder of bodice are done after smocking has been completed. If you use a gingham, striped or spotted fabric, where the pattern of the print can be used as a guide for spacing even gathers, you won't need a smocking dot pattern or grid.

1. Enlarge pattern pieces; cut paper pattern (see p. 126). Press fabric; using paper pattern, cut collar, sleeves and cuffs from fabric. Cut back and front rectangles from fabric, as specified on cutting diagram for size you are making (do not use paper bodice pattern). Prepare wrong side of fabric area indicated by smocking grid for gathering, using iron-on smocking spot transfer or Trace Erase™ grid (see p. 125). Leave ⅝" free for seams on three sides.

2. Thread needle with more than enough sewing or quilting thread to complete a line. Begin at right-hand side with a knot and a backstitch to secure thread firmly. Using dot pattern or grid as a guide, run gathering thread across first row at top; leave thread hanging at end of row. Repeat row every five squares or dots below.

3. When all gathering threads are in place, lay fabric flat on table and pull up on threads in pairs so that folds lie smoothly together like tubes. Secure threads by twisting each pair around a pin placed at end of row. Lay paper pattern for bodice on gathered piece and with contrasting thread, baste outline of pattern. Smock only within this area.

4. With blue embroidery floss, beginning at left at point just

Cutting diagrams

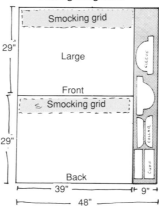

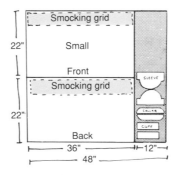

below neck, work a row of chevron stitch, four stitches up and four down; repeat last row directly underneath. Work another row of chevron stitch, four stitches down and four up, creating a diamond pattern; repeat last row directly underneath. Repeat last four rows three times, evenly spaced down yoke.

5. Measure width of front yoke; mark center point with pin. Measuring about ½" on either side of pin, cut slit 1" long in fold of gathers, centered between smocked bands. Cutting in fold of gathers, working from central

slits, cut a series of slits evenly spaced about 1" apart across yoke (actual measurement determined by size you are making). Weave grosgrain ribbon loosely through slits; lightly mark centers of areas of ribbon that show.

Actual–size embroidery design

6. Remove ribbon; transfer actual-size butterfly embroidery design to ribbon at each place marked (see p. 126). Using two strands of embroidery floss, stitch butterfly wings in long and short stitch; work body in a single bullion knot; head in a french knot, antennae in stem stitch and dot on wing in a french knot (see p. 119 for stitches). Weave embroidered ribbon through slits, centering butterflies. Stitch ribbon in place with small tacking stitches in folds of gathers. Repeat with a second ribbon between next bands of smocking.

7. Once gathers are drawn up on back yoke, work on wrong side of fabric. Stitch rows of cable stitch straight across back yoke, spaced every ¾"; this secures gathers without showing any smocking stitches on right side.

8. Carefully cut along basted line that marks center back of dress; line runs from neckline to bottom of smocked area. Right sides facing, join a 2" strip of fabric to each side for neck closing; fold back

and hem each side. Sew buttons ½" in on right side facing you; make buttonloops on opposite side. Join side seams and shoul- ders. Gather sleeve at top and bottom; join cuff. Sew in sleeves and sew on collar. Run embroidery floss through edges of eye- let on collar and cuffs, going in one hole and out next; turn up hem. Adjust gathers to lie flat and even; remove gathering stitches and steam smocking.

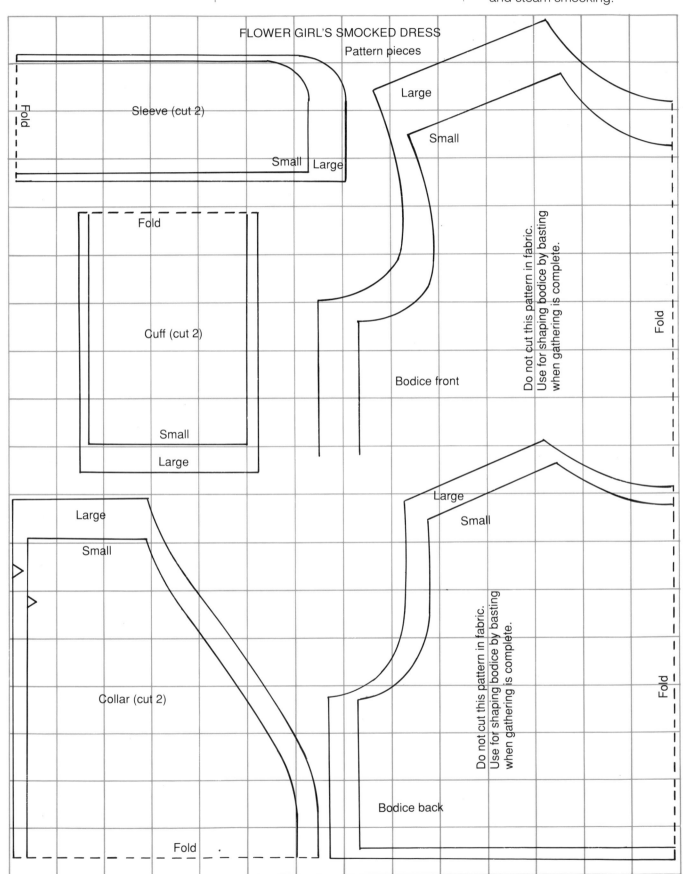

FLOWER GIRL'S SMOCKED DRESS
Pattern pieces

Sleeve (cut 2)

Fold

Large

Small

Small | Large

Cuff (cut 2)

Fold

Small

Large

Do not cut this pattern in fabric.
Use for shaping bodice by basting
when gathering is complete.

Bodice front

Fold

Large

Small

Large

Small

Collar (cut 2)

Do not cut this pattern in fabric.
Use for shaping bodice by basting
when gathering is complete.

Fold

Bodice back

Fold

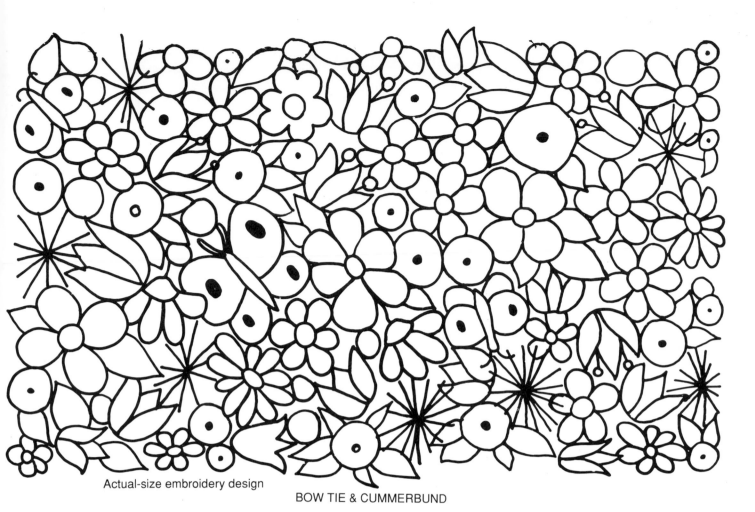

Actual-size embroidery design

BOW TIE & CUMMERBUND

EMBROIDERED BOW TIE AND CUMMERBUND
(Photo on p. 31)

Purchased black cummerbund
  and bow tie
Fine black muslin, ½ yard
Six-strand cotton embroidery
  floss in desired colors
Embroidery needle and hoop
Trace Erase™ fabric
Fine-tipped permanent marker

Erica *Using the Trace Erase™ fabric allows you to work with easy-to-follow outlines on dark fabrics. After finishing the embroidery, you simply tear away the web. Work from a brilliant palette of hues, as pictured, or use any color scheme you like.*

1. Carefully unpick lining of purchased tie and cummerbund. Stretch muslin in embroidery hoop or frame; baste tie and center front area of cummerbund face up on top. Trace actual-size design shown below onto webbing (see p. 126); lay over areas to be embroidered.

2. Using two strands of embroidery floss and working right through all layers, refer to color photo or your own color scheme and embroider all flowers and leaves in padded satin stitch; star flowers in bullion knots; flower centers in french knots and some leaves in fishbone stitch for variety (see p. 119).

3. When stitching is completed, tear away web, rubbing with flat points of scissors to remove unwanted bits and pieces. Trim away excess muslin. Press face down into a thick towel without stretching. Stitching with right sides together, reline cummerbund and tie, leaving a small opening; turn right side out and slipstitch opening closed.

FLOWERED HEADDRESS
(Photo on p. 32)

Plain elastic headband circle
1"-wide double-faced ivory satin
  ribbon, 10 yards
Matching sewing thread
Nylon monofilament
Seed pearl beads to fit snugly on
  monofilament without shifting
Very fine net tulle, 15 yards
⅜"-wide single-faced ivory satin
  ribbon, 1 yard

1. Cover plain headband circle with double-faced ribbon; seam to inside. Make and join 20 ruffled roses around headband: For each rose, gather lower edge of 6" length of double-faced ribbon, drawing up in a spiral; stitch firmly in place, referring to photo.

91

2. Cut 10" length of monofilament; thread three or four beads on one end; sew through headband between roses; thread three or four more beads on opposite end of monofilament, forming a sort of pearl antenna; cut off excess; repeat as desired.

3. Fold tulle in half crosswise; run a gathering thread across four inches down from fold. Gather tightly; stitch in place at back of band. Line headdress with single-faced ribbon.

EMBROIDERED BALLET SLIPPERS
(Photo on p. 32)

1 pair white ballet slippers
Lightweight even-weave
    fabric white to match, ¼ yard
Embroidery hoop and needle
Six-strand cotton embroidery floss
    in light pink, dark pink and green
Iron-on lightweight interfacing
Fabric glue

1. Mount fabric into embroidery hoop. Using two strands of embroidery floss, refer to actual-size embroidery design and color photo and embroider six or more rose clusters spaced at least 1" apart. Work roses in light pink and dark pink french knots, work stems in green straight stitches and leaves in green lazy daisy stitch (see p. 119 for stitches).

2. When stitching is completed, iron interfacing to reverse side of fabric, covering interfacing with foil before ironing so it will adhere only to back of fabric and embroidery. Using sharp scissors and being careful not to snip embroidery stitches, cut out rose clusters. Glue clusters to toe area of shoe, or where desired.

BALLET SLIPPERS
Actual-size embroidery design

EMBROIDERED SHOE BOWS
(Photo on p. 32)

Finished size: 1 ½" x 2"
1 pair shoes
Trace Erase ™ pen or fine-tipped
    permanent marker
Linen or fine even-weave cotton
    to match shoes, ¼ yard
Embroidery hoop and needle
Six-strand cotton embroidery floss
    in light pink, medium pink, dark
    pink, light blue, turquoise,
    green and light yellow or colors
    as desired
Fusible webbing
Fabric glue

1. With Trace Erase ™ pen or permanent marker, outline two 3" x 6" rectangles on fabric. Transfer actual-size bouquet design (shown below) to the center of each rectangle; do not cut out; mount into embroidery hoop.

SHOE BOWS

Actual-size embroidery design

2. Using two strands of embroidery floss and referring to color photo, embroider design: upper roses in bullion knots, lower rose and small flowers in french knots, leaves in lazy daisy stitch and bow in vertical satin stitch.

3. Cut out each embroidered

fabric rectangle; cut two rectangles of fusible webbing 1 ¼" x 3"; center behind embroidery and fold turnbacks over webbing to reverse side, leaving motif

exposed with no extra material above or below embroidery, and ¼" on either side. Press face down into a towel. Take a pleat so second fold projects ¼" beyond first on either side of the fabric to meet at back; press, secure with glue or double-edged tape; glue or stitch in place on front of shoe.

Erica You can also apply the bouquet directly to a satin pump, instead of onto a bow: When stitching is completed, iron lightweight interfacing to reverse side of fabric, covering interfacing with foil so it will adhere only to back of fabric and embroidery. Being careful not to snip embroidery, cut out each motif; glue to toe of shoe.

BRIDAL FAN
(Photo on p. 34)

Heavy stem wire
White florist's tape
2 ½"-wide lace, 2 ½ yards
⅝"-wide lace, 7 yards
Matching sewing thread
1 ½"-wide Offray single-faced
    satin ribbon, 5 yards
⅞"-wide Offray single-faced satin
    ribbon, 5 yards
6"-wide tulle, 3 yards
Baby's breath flowers
Silk ivy leaves and small flowers
Wire
Hot glue gun
Small pearls

Erica Decorative finishing may be stitched onto the fan instead of glued.

1. To make frame, twist to join pieces of stem wire until long enough to form fan shape of desired size (fig. A). Twist together at bottom to form handle; fold back; secure with florist's tape. To neaten ends and provide firmness, wrap entire frame with florist's tape.

2. Sew four pieces of 2 ½"-wide lace together along long edges

BRIDAL FAN

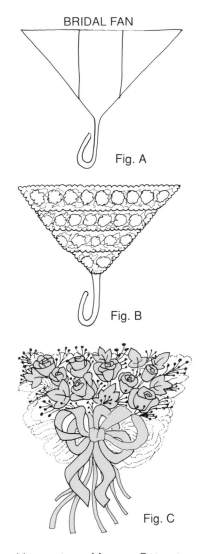

Fig. A

Fig. B

Fig. C

and lay on top of frame. Cut out lace sized to frame leaving bottom edge slightly wider; baste edges of lace to frame, gathering at bottom (fig. B). Finish by sewing strip of ⅝" lace around all edges to cover frame.

3. Make assorted ribbon roses from satin ribbons (see p. 124). Cut tulle in 6" x 6" squares; pinch at center; wrap pinch of fabric with wire and then with florist's tape. Make various loops with ⅞" ribbon; secure base of each loop by wrapping with wire and florist's tape. Arrange loops, tulle, roses, baby's breath, small silk flowers and ivy leaves on fan (see photo and fig. C); glue in place with hot glue gun.

4. Make streamers from lace and satin; make bows from tulle and lace; glue to bottom of fan. Cover all exposed wire with florist's tape. Scatter small pearls over fan; glue in place.

LACE COLLAGE YOKE
(Photo on p. 35)

Purchased blouse and skirt pattern
Tracing paper
Muslin
Nylon net or tulle
Wright's lace as follows (or your own arrangement of lace):
    7 ½"-wide flat Chantilly galloon
    4 ½"-wide flat Chantilly galloon
    2 ⅜"-wide embroidered net scalloped swagg
    2" Venetian lace trim
    3 Venetian lace medallions
    1 ¼"-wide Valenciennes ruffled lace
Handkerchief linen, sufficient quantity to complete dress (about 4-6 yards)
Clear nylon thread
Matching sewing thread
RIT dye, or dyeing crystals in desired color

Erica *Make yoke using pattern shown below, or purchased pattern in whatever shape you desire. Preshrink fabric and dye all materials as yardage before starting. Man-made fibers accept dye differently from natural ones, so test-dye some of your materials before committing the complete yardage. Follow dye manufacturer's instructions. Soft shades such as stonewashed blue (pictured), toast, coral or pistachio are available and will give a unique look. A slight tone variation is attractive. The dress pictured was made from a Vogue pattern (see suppliers, p. 128).*

1. Enlarge yoke pattern on tracing paper (see p. 126); use paper pattern to cut out yoke in muslin. Fit yoke on figure or dressmaker's dummy; arrange lace pieces face down on top of muslin, referring to color photo and to drawing below for lace placement or creating your own arrangement. When you find the arrangement you like, pin or tape lace in position.

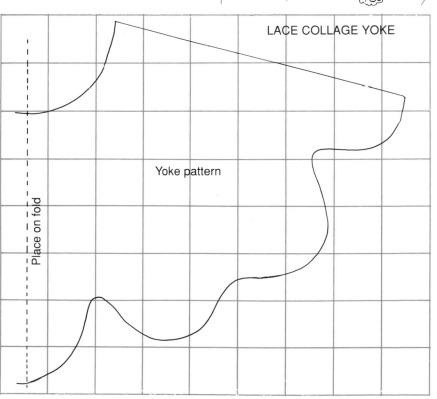

LACE COLLAGE YOKE

Place on fold

Yoke pattern

93

2. Cut yoke from nylon tulle; overlay on lace collage. Pin and invisibly stitch lace to tulle from the back, using clear nylon thread and being careful not to stitch through to muslin. Remove basting stitches or tape and turn yoke inside out. Lace will be joined to tulle. Finish with lace stand-up collar, edging with gathered lace ruffle; join to dress bodice.

3. Make up blouse and skirt following pattern instructions.

WHITE-ON-WHITE EMBROIDERED BRIDAL GOWN

(Photo on p. 36)

Purchased patterns for back-but= toning blouse (optional) and petticoat
Tracing paper or shelf paper
Trace Erase™ pen or hard pencil
100% cotton, lawn, batiste or fine-weave muslin fabric, sufficient to make up blouse and skirt
Matching sewing thread
Embroidery frame
Lace for bodice: 1"-wide bands crochet lace, antique lace pieces, wide lace that can be cut into narrow bands, or lace insertion
Lace for skirt, hem and collar and cuffs of bodice: 1"-wide insertion lace and 1 ¾"-wide lace edging
Six-strand white cotton embroidery floss
No. 8 or 9 crewel needle
Straight pins and sharp scissors

Erica The gown pictured was made from a Vogue pattern (see suppliers, p. 128). Use a purchased pattern for both blouse and skirt, or enlarge blouse pattern shown, using your back waist measurement as a sizing guide.

1. Enlarge and trace embroidery patterns onto layout paper (see p. 126). Using Trace Erase™ pen,

Embroidery designs   WHITE-ON-WHITE GOWN

Collar

Back

Front

hard pencil or basting stitches, outline blouse pattern pieces on batiste. Do not cut out (to avoid stretching, do not cut out fabric pieces until embroidery is finished). With hard pencil or Trace Erase™ pen, transfer embroidery designs to batiste within pattern outlines. Mount batiste rectangles in embroidery frame (see p. 126).

2. Baste lace insertion in positions marked by long vertical bands on embroidery pattern. With crewel needle and single strand of embroidery floss, buttonhole lace in position (see p. 119 for stitches) with loops to outside (if you prefer, join lace by

hand using whipstitch or point de Paris (p. 125), or by machine using entre deux or overlock stitch). Repeat to join round circles on top of each vertical band.

3. When stitching is complete, working on the reverse side, separate lace from the batiste of the bodice by inserting a pair of crossed pins between the two layers. Where the pins cross, insert points of scissors and make the first small snip. Working from this point, carefully cut away the batiste behind the lace close against the edge. (The crossed pins insure that you will not accidentally snip the lace with your

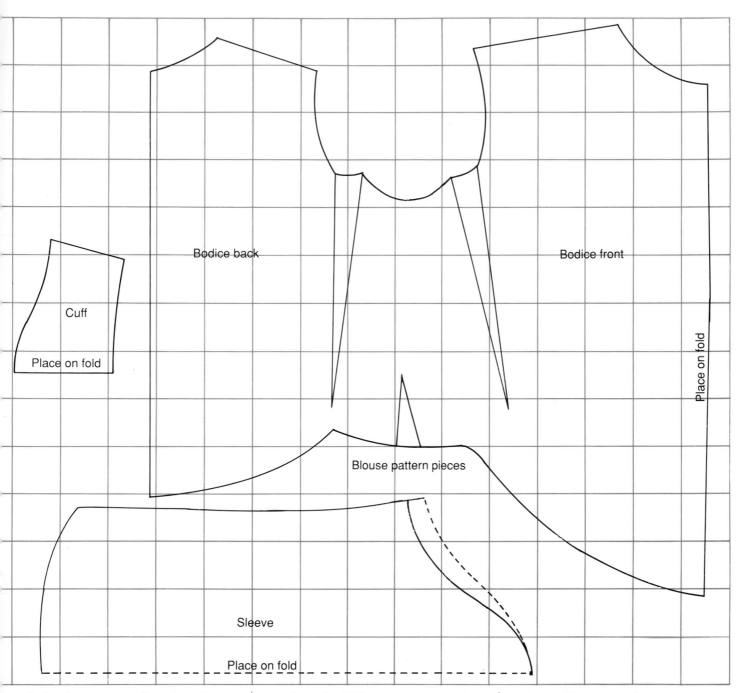

Cuff

Place on fold

Bodice back

Bodice front

Place on fold

Blouse pattern pieces

Sleeve

Place on fold

first cut; as you continue to cut, you can separate the two layers with your fingers.)

4. Make eyelets in center of each flower by piercing a small hole with a sharp scissors and button-hole-stitching around it, loops to outside. As you work, rotate nee-dle in hole to keep it open. Work center of large central flower in same way. Using two strands of floss, embroider all circles, leaves and motifs in padded satin stitch. Work eyelets and embroidery on back of bodice, sleeves, collar and cuffs in same manner. Make up blouse with entre deux seams and, if desired, hand-covered

buttons (p 125).

5. Make two flounced ruffles for skirt as follows. Cut two bands 10" x 5 yards from batiste. Apply lace edging to bottom of bands by turning up narrow hem to right side and machine-stitching lace edging on top. Apply insertion lace 1" above lower border, machine-stitching on both edges. Carefully cut away batiste from reverse side of insertion lace in same manner as step 3. Clean-finish upper edge of flounce by making narrow hem; machine-stitch two lines of gathering close to upper edge. Clean-finish hem of skirt (10" shorter than final hem)

by making narrow hem.

6. Cut brown paper pattern same length as skirt circumference; along length of pattern, rule two parallel lines as far apart as inser-tion lace is wide. Baste gathered flounce to paper pattern along lower line; baste clean-finished hem of skirt to paper pattern along upper line. Machine-stitch along both edges of insertion lace, catching hem on one edge, ruffle on the other. Tear away paper; repeat step 6 to join upper ruffle. Following pattern instruc-tions, make up skirt.

SHADOW-STITCH EMBROIDERY FOR YOUR BRIDAL GOWN

(Photo on p. 37)

Purchased gown pattern with
  gathered, bloused sleeves and
  buttoning cuffs
Fabrics and notions to make gown
60"-wide organdy to match gown
  fabric, 1 ½ yards
Shelf paper or tracing paper
Fine felt-tipped permanent marker
Trace Erase™ pen or hard pencil
Embroidery frame and needle
Six-strand white cotton embroi-
  dery floss
Small pearl buttons for cuffs

Erica   *Shadow work, a close herringbone stitch worked on the reverse
side of fabric, gives a soft, light effect.
The finer and closer your stitching, the
whiter and crisper your finished result.
Since organdy is transparent, take care
to begin and end all embroidery stitching
invisibly, keep your seams neat and narrow and your stitches tiny, as they will
be visible from the right side. Neat
seams may be made by machine-over-
casting raw edges first, then seaming
right sides together close to edge, or
making french seams. The dress pictured
was made from a Vogue pattern (see
suppliers, p. 128).*

1. Mark organdy into generous
rectangles within which you can
outline pattern pieces for dress
bodice, sleeves and cuffs (or
whichever parts of dress you
wish to embroider). With basting
stitches, outline pieces within
rectangles. Do not cut out pattern
pieces at this time: Cut out rectangles only. Set aside cuffs.

2. Enlarge embroidery design on
paper (see p. 126). Extend
design in all directions, continuing and reversing motifs as
desired for a flowing, airy look.
Outline design with permanent
marker. Overlay design with
organdy rectangles, with sleeve
or other pattern piece outline
basted on top; use Trace Erase™
pen or hard pencil to trace
design onto organdy. To match
sleeves trace first sleeve, flip over
design and trace other side onto
second sleeve.

3. Mount fabric tautly, wrong side
up, into embroidery hoop or
frame (see p. 126). Using two
strands of embroidery floss,
embroider design in close herringbone stitch to create shadow
work (see p. 119 for stitches). Cut
out pattern pieces with turnbacks.

4. Stitch two rows of running
stitches along top and bottom
edges of sleeves. Right sides
together, fold cuffs in half widthwise; stitch along side and angu-
lar edges. Trim seam; turn to right
side. Right sides together (backstitch side is right side), fold
sleeves in half lengthwise; stitch
seam leaving 2" unstitched at
bottom edge; trim seam edge to
¼"; overcast to finish. Narrow-hem
unstitched 2" seam edge to finish. Turn sleeve to right side;
gather lower edge, pin cuff to fit
with right sides together and stitch.

5. Gather upper edge of sleeve
together, matching side seams of
dress bodice with sleeve seam;
pin in place, smoothing out fullness
so that all gathers are at shoulder;
stitch in place. Make buttonholes
on cuffs; stitch buttons in place to
correspond. Make up rest of dress
following pattern instructions.

SHADOW STITCH EMBROIDERY

Embroidery design

BEADED LACE FOR YOUR BRIDAL GOWN

(Photo on p. 39)

Lace to be applied to your bridal
  gown, or purchased bridal
  gown with lace areas
Pearl beads
Nylon beading thread
Beading needles
Vinyl shelf paper

*Erica Beads can be applied to any
lace area. Select pearl beads that closely
match the color of the fabric, or silver
or gold contrasting beads to create an
exciting accent on a neck, back or sleeve
edge, the collar, bodice, cuffs, sleeves,
train, etc. If stitching your own dress,
do your beading before applying the
lace; especially if the lace is to be used as
an overlay or in a difficult-to-stitch area.
Select a bead size that complements the
lace or fabric; stitch on following the
design of the lace. These directions apply
to any type of bead application. The
gown pictured was made using a Vogue
pattern (see suppliers, p. 128).*

1. Cut a piece of vinyl shelf
paper slightly larger than the area
to be beaded and baste the lace
to it (this gives a flimsy lace or
fabric a firm backing and makes
the beading easier; the needle
glances off the vinyl surface without catching). Thread your needle
with both ends of a doubled
thread. Take a small stitch into the
fabric and, when coming up,
thread the needle through the
loop at the end of the doubled
thread. Transfer beads onto needle from their original string.

BEADED LACE

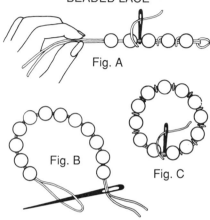

Fig. A

Fig. B

Fig. C

2. Sew beads down to lace rows,
or individually, ending off securely
with backstitches. Closely
spaced beads may first be strung
on double thread, then secured
with tiny couching stitches
placed between beads (fig. A).
To sew beads in a ring, complete
the circle by threading through
the loop (fig. B), then secure with
couching stitches (fig. C).

PEARL-EDGED BRIDAL GOWN

(Photo on p. 41)

Purchased wedding gown or pat-
  tern with low V-back
Fabrics and notions to make gown
Pearls
Quilting thread, waxed thread or
  clear nylon thread

*Erica The gown pictured was
made from a Vogue pattern (see suppliers, p. 128). Add beads to a ready-
made gown, or to one you make yourself from a purchased pattern, or enlarging the pattern given below, using your
back waist measurement as a guide.*

1. Follow pattern instructions to
make up dress. Using double
thread for strength, string
sufficient pearls to encircle entire
top of dress. Using quilting,
waxed or nylon thread, sew
pearls to extreme edge of fabric,
with tiny invisible couching stitches between pearls (fig. A).
Stretch string taut as you sew to
prevent rippling of the outer edge.

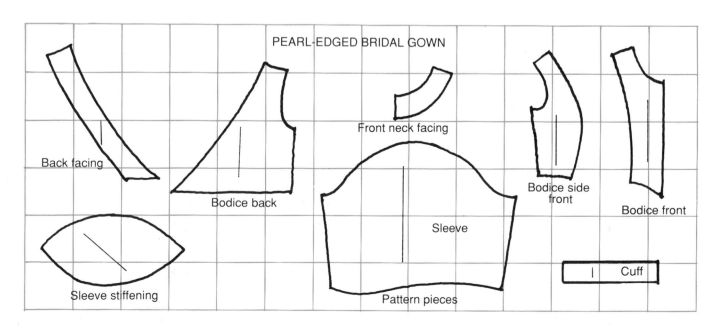

PEARL-EDGED BRIDAL GOWN

Back facing

Bodice back

Front neck facing

Sleeve

Bodice side front

Bodice front

Sleeve stiffening

Pattern pieces

Cuff

PEARL-WRAPPED HEAD-DRESS
(Photo on p. 41)
Pearls
Quilt batting
Large blunt needle
40"-wide fine tulle, 5 yards

1. From same fabric as dress, cut bias strip 3" wide; length of strip should be circumference of head plus 2" for padding with ⅜" seam allowance on all sides. Fold over lengthwise, right sides together; stitch along edge leaving ends open. Press open turn-backs and turn right side out.

2. Cut strip of batting double width and same length as fabric tube; roll neatly lengthwise. Attach a doubled thread to one end of roll; with large blunt needle, drop thread through fabric tube, pull batting inside. Wrap pearl rope diagonally to form a continuous spiral around padded tube; fit to head and slipstitch ends closed. Secure ends of pearl rope.

3. Cut 4 yards of 40"-wide tulle; double it over to measure 20". Along fold, work a double row of gathering threads; draw up 4-yard length to measure only 8". Join lightly inside center back of headdress. Cut 1 yard of matching tulle in half lengthwise; fold in thirds. Bunch together into three loops simulating a bow; sew closely together on outside of circle at center back of headdress.

PEARL-KNOTTED SHOES
(Photo on p. 40)
1 pair satin pumps, plain or decorated with pearl beads
Miniature pearls
Waxed button thread or clear nylon filament
Blunt tapestry needle

1. Tie string of pearls into double knot for each shoe. With fine, sharp needle or other instrument, puncture two tiny holes in shoe upper, either side of where you will place pearl knot. Thread tapestry needle with button thread or nylon; leaving end dangling, come up through one hole, catch pearl knot, go down through other hole; knot two ends together underneath. Trim ends of pearl string.

BEADED LACE, DETACH-ABLE BOW & BACK BUT-TON-FASTENING FOR YOUR BRIDAL GOWN
(Photo on p. 42)

Purchased dress pattern with train, lace trim, low back and back fastening
Satin, peau de soie, or taffeta, sufficient to make dress and train
Heavy lace backed with net
Pearl beads
Mother-of-pearl sequins
Nylon beading thread
Beading needle
Pearl buttons, four ½", one 1"
Six-strand cotton embroidery floss to match dress fabric
Organdy for back button panel
¼" pearl shank buttons for back button panel

Erica Gown shown was made from a Vogue pattern (see suppliers, p. 128).

1. Apply beads and sequins to lace for dress (see directions for beaded lace gown on p. 97). Make up dress following pattern instructions.

2. To make bow for train, using same fabric as dress, cut double fabric 2 yards by 10". Right sides together, sew on three sides, leaving one short end open, forming a long fabric cylinder. Press turnbacks open, turn right side out; slipstitch opening closed. Press and tie into a graceful bow with long ends. Secure bow with invisible stitches; sew large button to center back (see fig. A).

3. Establish point at center back of dress for fastening up train: Lift center of train to center back until train falls just to floor length, level with dress hem. With pins, mark the two points, one on train and one on dress; you will place buttonloops here for joining bow (loops will be invisible if you

place them in areas of lace).

4. Establish length of buttonloop by wrapping thread to slip easily over large button. With four

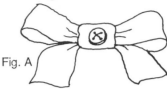

Fig. A

strands of embroidery floss, make a buttonhole loop at each marked point (one on dress, one on train): Holding one smaller size button behind dress on right side, come up through button and dress, go across horizontally and down slightly to left going through fabric and second smaller button held behind dress at left side. Come up on same side, through button and fabric again; repeat to make five long stitches same size as loop. Now work closely spaced buttonhole stitch over these long stitches back to starting point from left to right to complete first loop (see fig. B). Repeat step 4 to make second horizontal loop in position this way. (On completed dress, to pick up train simply button bow first through lower and then upper loop–small buttons in back will support weight of train without tearing dress fabric.)

Fig. B

5. To make back button-fastening, clean-finish both edges of organdy at back of bodice opening, making ⅜" hem; both sides will meet edge to edge. With four strands of embroidery floss, sew pearl shank buttons to right side ½" apart, taking two backstitches to secure each one, taking nee-

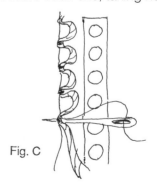

Fig. C

dle through hem to next without ending off thread for strength.

6. Cut ¼" bias strip of organdy to length of opening. Moisten finger and thumb, make a tight roll and secure with small slipstitches. Couch this roll on outer edge of left side of opening opposite buttons. Secure with two small vertical stitches, spaced between buttons. For strength, slide needle through roll to come out in position for next stitch along whole length of opening (fig. C).

WELCOME MAT
(Photo on p. 44)

Finished size: 22" x 24", plus fringe
Layout paper or shelf paper
No. 5 rug canvas, 28" x 30"

Permanent marker
Artist's stretcher strips, two 28" and two 30"
Staplegun or thumbtacks
Three-strand persian yarn or sport-weight knitting yarn (see color key)
No. 14 tapestry needle
Heavy open-weave fabric, 23" x 25" rectangle
Sport-weight yarn, 300 yards off-white for fringes (optional)
Crochet hook (optional)

1. Enlarge design on layout paper (see p. 126). Place design under canvas, aligning canvas threads with straight lines

Crewel motifs

Stitch Key

A., F., K. Vertical bargello (over two mesh)

B., C., O. Lazy daisy stitch

D. Buttonhole stitch

E., L. Straight stitch (radiating from center hole)

I. Outline stitch

J. French knot

K. Bargello (alternately over one and two mesh)

L., M., N. Satin or straight stitches

Detail of border stitches

Color key

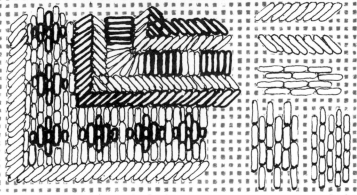

1 2 3 4
5 6 7 8
9 10 11 12
13 14

of design, and trace outlines with permanent marker. Staple or tack canvas onto stretcher strip frame (see p. 126).

2. Working with three strands of yarn, fill in garden and house areas of design with vertical bargello stitches over 2 mesh of the canvas, following chart (see p. 122 for needlepoint). When all bargello stitching is complete, work outline stitch around each area, using one strand of yarn, rounding out floral areas and sharpening straight edges.

3. Embroider details on top of needlepoint: With one strand of yarn work floral motifs and white trim on house (see p. 119).

4. Stitch border: Beginning at the edges of the picture and working outward, follow the border stitch diagrams and work four narrow bands of color as shown, then work a wide band of white with diamond pattern and the word "welcome"; finish with a last narrow band of color.

5. Block needlepoint (see p. 119). When dry, turn canvas edges under, mitering corners; sew miters together. Mount on backing fabric. To add fringe, cut strands of off-white yarn 12" long; separate into groups of four strands. Fold strands in half; using crochet hook, pull loop from front to back through mesh at edge of mat; bring fringe ends through loop and pull up to tighten. Trim fringe evenly.

STRAWBERRY TOASTER COVER
(Photo on p. 46)

Print fabric of your choice
10-mesh Trace Erase™ grid
Embroidery hoop or frame
Six-strand cotton embroidery floss
   (see color key)
White pearl cotton
Embroidery needle
Matching sewing thread
Matching piping and bias binding

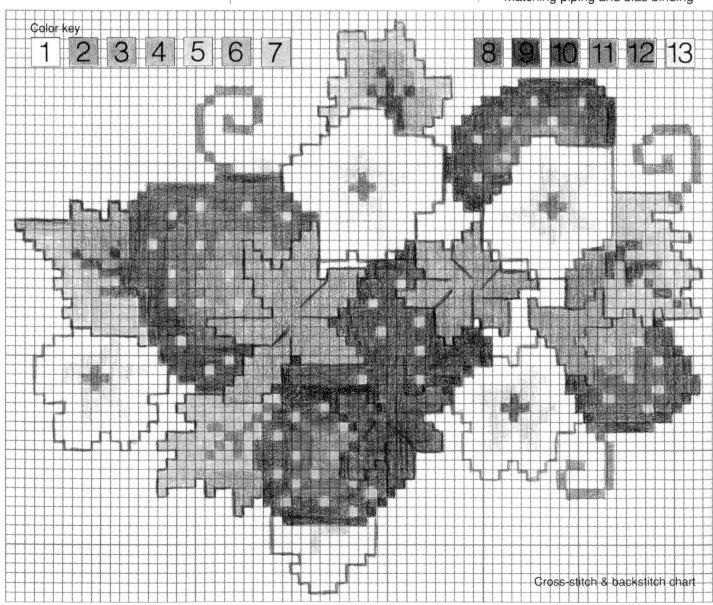

Color key

1 2 3 4 5 6 7   8 9 10 11 12 13

Cross-stitch & backstitch chart

Erica *Cross stitch can be worked on any fabric when you use the Trace Erase™ grid to guide your stitches. Simply baste the grid on top of the fabric and then follow the chart. If you prefer working without the Trace Erase™ grid, use 10-mesh even-weave fabric. This design would also be pretty decorating a tablemat, apron, tie-on chair seat or as a kitchen picture.*

1. Stretch fabric right side up in embroidery hoop or frame. Baste Trace Erase™ grid in position on top of fabric. Using three strands of embroidery floss and single strand of unseparated pearl cotton, follow chart and cross stitch flowers and leaves, working right through both layers (see p. 119 for stitches).

2. Using backstitch and three strands of floss, outline flowers in pink and leaves in dark green. When stitching is complete, keep fabric in hoop and briskly tear away Trace Erase™. Pulling toward the stitches results in a cleaner tear. Remove any remaining bits and pieces by carefully rubbing with blunt edge of scissors or using tweezers.

3. Measure height and width of your toaster; draw paper pattern for back and front; cut from fabric, keeping embroidery centered. Cut fabric strip for gusset to run between back and front. Baste piping in position around edges of back and front, with right sides together and raw edges even; join long edges of gusset to back and front; stitch and turn right side out. Finish with bias binding to match piping.

FOLK DOLL MAGNET

(Photo on p. 46)

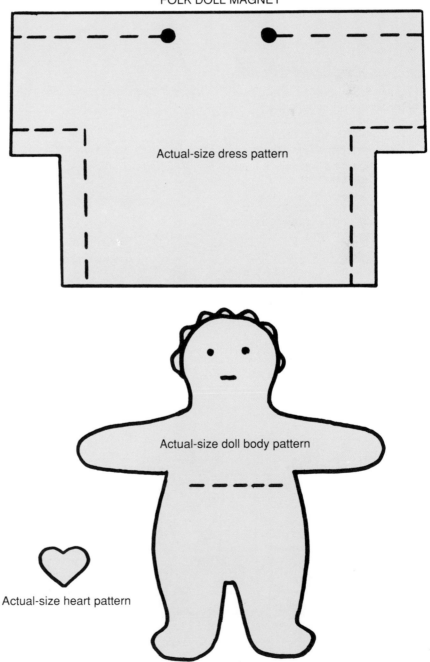

Muslin, 4" x 8" piece for body
Small-print calico, 3" x 7" piece for dress

Matching sewing thread
Polyester fiberfill, small amount
Six-strand cotton embroidery
    floss, few yards brown
Scrap of red felt
½"-diameter round magnet
White glue

1. Right sides together, fold muslin in half; transfer pattern for body onto one side of fabric (see p. 126). Using small machine-stitches, stitch through both layers along traced outline. Trim seam to ⅛", clip curves and slash body at chest through one layer only. Turn right side out through

slashed opening and stuff; insert magnet; slipstitch opening closed. With three strands of floss, work french knot eyes, straight-stitch mouth and bullion-stitch hair (see p. 119).

2. Right sides together, fold calico in half; transfer actual-size dress pattern to wrong side of fabric; cut out dress front and back. Stitch together at underarm and shoulder seams, leaving open at neck edge between dots. Clip corners and to dots in seam allowance; turn right side out and narrow-hem lower edge

FOLK DOLL MAGNET

Actual-size dress pattern

Actual-size doll body pattern

Actual-size heart pattern

$3.$ Place dress on doll. Turn raw neck and sleeve edges in ¼"; gather and stitch sleeves to wrists. Pleat and stitch dress at either side of neck opening and sleeve edges. Cut heart from felt and glue to doll's hand.

DUCK, CAT & SCOTTY DOG MAGNETS
(Photo on p. 46)

Fabric scraps, cotton or cotton-blend small prints, checks, plaids and calicoes
Polyester fiberfill, small amount
½"-diameter round magnets, one for each
⅛"-wide Offray satin ribbon, 8" each for Duck and Cat
⅜"-wide Offray satin ribbon, plaid or striped, 9" for Scotty
Matching sewing threads

$1.$ Transfer design to wrong side of fabric (see p. 126). Right sides together, using small machine stitches, stitch through both layers along traced outline, leaving opening between dots. Trim seam allowance to ⅛"; clip corners and curves and turn right side out. Stuff and insert magnet; slipstitch opening and tie ribbon bow around neck.

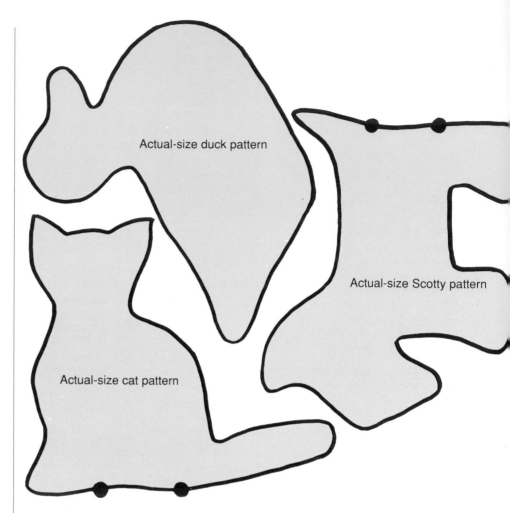

Actual-size duck pattern

Actual-size Scotty pattern

Actual-size cat pattern

TEA COSY COTTAGE
(Photo on p. 47)

Finished size: about 11" x 5", plus gables and chimney
36"-wide calico fabric, ½ yard each white and yellow
Lining fabric, ½ yard
Scrap of red calico
Tracing paper
Batting
Six-strand cotton embroidery floss in black, pink, yellow, blue and three shades of green
Embroidery needle and hoop or frame

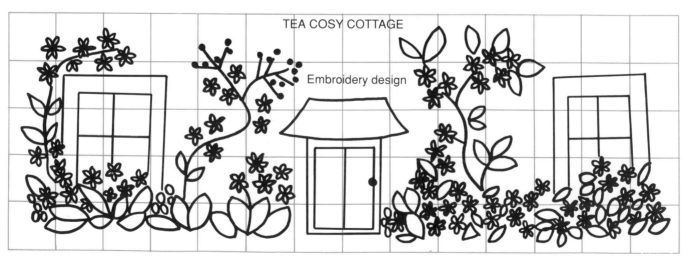

TEA COSY COTTAGE

Embroidery design

1. From white calico, cut cottage front and back, each 6" high and 12" wide. Cut two 5" x 9" gables; fold each in half lengthwise. Starting 4" from bottom, draw slightly curved line to top (center fold); cut on drawn line and open. From yellow calico, cut roof 14" deep and 15" wide. From red calico, cut 5" x 8" chimney. From lining fabric, cut two 8" x 16" pieces.

2. On tracing paper, draw a 4" x 10" rectangle. Draw seam allowance ½" from top long edge. Referring to embroidery design below (you may enlarge and trace it exactly if you like; see p. 126) draw cottage door, centered and resting on bottom line; draw windows and vines; draw leaves ½" long or less. Transfer drawing to fabric for cottage front, with top edge matching top line and centered between side edges.

3. Place white calico in embroidery hoop. With full six strands of embroidery floss, outline doors and windows, filling in with black long and short stitch. Work satin-stitch leaves in greens; work pink and yellow lazy daisy stitch flowers with yellow french knot centers. Scatter blue french knots (see p. 119 for stitches).

4. Baste batting to back of each fabric piece, except lining. Right sides together, seam roof, centered between cottage back and front, stopping ¾" from each end; turn under 2 ½" at each seamed edge of roof and stitch across ends (fig. A). Bring in side of roof to match side of cottage (extra fabric will form pleat at top edge); stitch down side edges, through all layers; stitch across top edge through the pleat.

5. Fold chimney in half (2 ½" x 8") and seam three edges, leaving an opening to turn. Turn right side out; turn in open edges and slipstitch. Sew ends of chimney 2" apart to center of roof, forming a handle. Gables: Seam a gable at each end of cottage, matching center of gable to center of roof. Turn right side out.

6. Right sides together, seam lining pieces together at two short ends and one long end. Turn up 1 ½" at bottom edge of cottage;

slide lining inside, with a seam at center of each end. Turn raw edge under; slipstitch to cottage all around bottom.

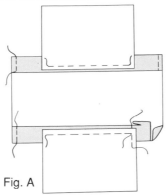

Fig. A

MOSS HEART WREATH
(*Photo on p. 46*)

Finished size: about 14" across
Wire hanger
Pliers
Spanish moss
Spray glue adhesive
⅛"-wide pink floral fused-edge grosgrain ribbon
Dried baby's breath
Dried rosebuds (flowers and leaves)
Old pencil
Newspaper
Rubber gloves

Erica Most materials are available at florist's supply stores.

1. Enlarge heart pattern (see p. 126). Using pattern as a guide, with pliers cut off hook of hanger and bend wire into heart shape; hook ends together at heart top center. Cut a 6" piece from remaining wire to use later for wreath hanger.

2. Cover work area with newspaper and use gloves to protect hands while using spray adhesive. Pull out long portions of moss and wrap around wire heart, shaping moss with hands and spraying with adhesive to hold moss together. Continue wrapping, spraying and shaping moss around wire until uniformly about 3" thick; fill in sparse areas with small amounts of moss.

3. Make a 1" loop at one end of 6" wire; stick straight wire end through moss at heart top center from back to front; bend around to back, winding end around loop

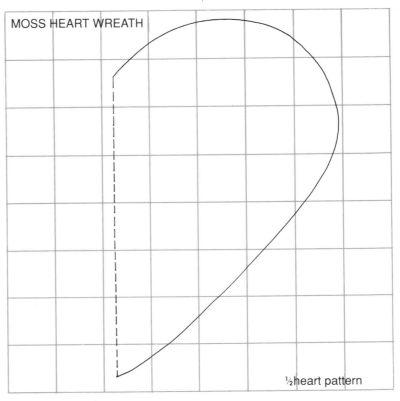

MOSS HEART WREATH

½ heart pattern

base to form wreath hanger. Patch moss in front as necessary.

4. Wind and criss-cross ribbon around moss heart, using color photo as guide and securing ends at back. Make a double-looped ribbon bow; glue to heart top center. Make small bouquets of baby's breath; with pencil, poke holes in moss at top center heart near bow and on either side of heart; spray adhesive into hole and insert bouquet. Spray and arrange dried rosebuds and leaves around baby's breath and in moss as desired.

STENCILED BED PILLOW
(Photo on p. 48)

Clear acetate
X-acto knife or hot knife
Masking tape
Stencil paints in desired colors
Stenciling brushes
White cotton broadcloth, 1 yard
Embroidery hoop or frame
Six-strand cotton embroidery floss
Crewel and quilting needles
Quilt batting
Artist's stretcher strips
Staplegun or tacks
Soft muslin backing fabric, 1 yard
Small-print fabric, ½ yard
Polyester fiberfill or pillow form

1. Enlarge stenciling design to desired size (see p. 126). Tape acetate in place on top of design; with X-acto knife or hot knife, cut out stencil.

2. Lay broadcloth on firm, smooth surface; center stencil on top of fabric and tape in place. Select first color and cover other areas with tape. Working with completely dry stencil brush (no water), stipple paint onto fabric, working more closely around edge than in the center of each stencil shape (see p. 126 for stenciling tips); repeat with other colors, one at a time.

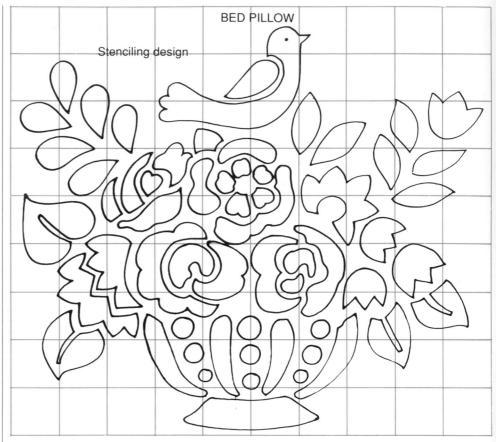

BED PILLOW

Stenciling design

3. When paint is completely dry, embellish stenciling with embroidery details. Mount fabric into embroidery hoop or frame; using three strands of embroidery floss work fly stitch on bird's body; using full six strands, work french knots in center of flowers (see p. 119 for stitches).

4. Place quilt batting behind stenciled fabric. Place backing fabric behind batting; baste layers firmly together using wide basting stitch. Secure to stretcher strip frame with staples or tacks (see p. 126), leaving fabric slack enough so that four or five stitches can be taken at one time on the needle. With quilting thread and needle, use running stitch to quilt just outside outlines of stenciled shapes (see p. 123 for quilting). Trim and mount pillow (see p. 123), edging with contrasting print fabric, doubled over and mitered at corners.

Erica *This design works well as a large European square, surrounded with smaller pillows on a bed, or adding coziness to a sofa or easy chair.*

FRILLED BOLSTER
(Photo on p. 48)
Finished size: 18" long and about 4 ½" in diameter
Small-print fabric (A), ½ yard
Coordinating floral print fabric (B), ½ yard
⅛"-wide matching satin ribbon, 1 ½ yards
1"-wide pre-gathered ivory eyelet trim, 1 yard
Matching sewing threads
Polyester fiberfill or bolster form

Erica *Use ½" seams throughout unless otherwise indicated.*

1. Cut one 12" x 14" rectangle and two 4" x 14" rectangles from fabric A. Cut two 8" x 24" rectangles from fabric B. With right sides together, sew together long edges of large fabric A rectangle to form a tube; trim seam and turn right side out.

2. For ruffles, with right sides together, stitch together short ends of one fabric B rectangle to form a ring; turn right side out; fold ring in half lengthwise. Stitch two rows of gathering stitches along unfinished edge. Repeat

with other fabric rectangle. Cut eyelet lace trim into two lengths; baste one to each raw edge of fabric A tube; gathering to fit, pin one fabric B ruffle over lace to same edge at each end; stitch in place.

3. To make endpieces, stitch together short edges of one remaining rectangle, leaving about 2" unstitched along one end; clean-finish remainder of seam. Press long edge closest to unstitched edge under 1" to wrong side; fold and press again ½" from edge. Stitch close to interior folded edge to form casing. Repeat with last rectangle. With right sides together and raw edges even, stitch one to each end of bolster tube on top of ruffles, being careful to match seam lines. Cut ribbon into two lengths; thread one through each casing. Stuff pillow firmly; draw casing closed and tie with bow.

BEANBAG BED TRAY
(Photo on p.48)

Finished size: 10 ½" x 13" or desired size

10 ½" x 13" plastic tray, or tray of desired size
Large floral-print fabric (A), ½ yard
Small floral-print fabric (B), ½ yard
Muslin, 1 yard
Matching sewing thread
Clear polyurethane and brush
Fabric glue
4 Velcro™ fasteners
2 large buttons
Small Styrofoam™ balls

Erica Cover your tray with pre-printed fabric, or stencil a plain fabric with any design you like.

1. Cut 17" x 14 ½" rectangle from large-print fabric. Glue to tray front; turn edges to back. or glue over edge of tray (to facilitate turning fabric over corners, after saturating with glue, gather fabric with fingers at corners of tray and cut notches from fabric before turning). Paint covered tray with polyurethane.

2. To make pillow pattern, draw on paper a rectangle same size as tray plus 1 ½" all around; notch corners 1 ½" and draw two diagonals across (see fig. A); cut out all four pieces of pattern.

Use pattern to cut two of each piece from small-print fabric and from muslin.

3. Join small-print fabric sections along diagonals to form pillow front; repeat for back. Right sides, together, seam corners to form box shape on back and front; join back and front, leaving one side open for stuffing. Repeat in muslin for pillow liner; stuff liner with Styrofoam™ balls and stitch opening closed. Insert liner; sew pillow opening closed.

4. Cover two buttons with small-print fabric (see p. 125); sew one above, one below pillow, pulling tightly to firmly gather in center (fig. B). Sew Velcro™ fasteners to four corners of pillow; glue to corners on tray; fasten (fig. C).

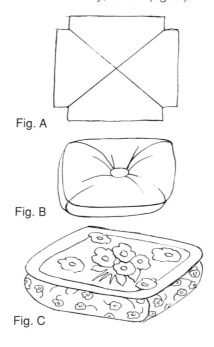

Fig. A

Fig. B

Fig. C

TRAY WITH HANGER
(Photo on p. 49)

Plastic tray, 13 ½" x 18" or desired size
Large floral-print fabric, ¾ yard
Coordinating small floral-print fabric, ½ yard

Matching sewing thread
Polyester batting
Fabric glue
Spray-on fabric stiffener
Clear polyurethane and brush
18" wooden dowel
Velcro™ fasteners (optional)

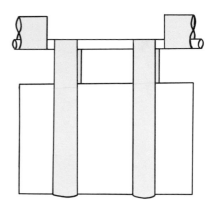

1. Cut large-print fabric 3" larger than tray all around; glue to front of tray, turning edges over tray rim (after saturating with glue, gather fabric with fingers at corners of tray; cut notches from fabric at corners to facilitate turning); let dry thoroughly; spray with fabric stiffener; let dry. Coat with polyurethane; let dry.

2. Cut rectangles from small-print fabric: four 10 ½" x 2 ⅝", four 36" x 2 ⅝", four 10 ½" x 1 ½" and four 36" x 1 ½". Cut the following rectangles from batting: two 10 ½" x 2 ⅝" and two 36" x 2 ⅝". Right sides facing out, sandwich each batting rectangle between two same-size fabric rectangles. Machine- or hand-quilt as desired (see p. 123).

3. Press long edges of remaining fabric strips ½" to wrong side. Wrong sides together, fold in half lengthwise; press. Encase long edges of quilted rectangles with se strips; stitch in place ... ough all thicknesses, close to ½" folded edge.

4. Slipstitch raw edges of each rectangle together, neatly turning edges under, to form a cylinder. Stitch through all thicknesses, 2 ½" from one short edge. Slip quilted rectangles onto dowel, as shown in color photo. Slip tray into hangers. Hang dowel on door or wall. If desired, fasten tray to hangers with Velcro™ fasteners.

NEEDLEPOINT COTTAGE
Needlepoint design

Color key  A B C D E F G H I J K L M

NEEDLEPOINT ROSE-COVERED COTTAGE
(Photo on p. 50)

Finished design size: 6" x 10"
Finished picture size: 9" x 12"
Layout paper
14-mesh needlepoint canvas, ½ yard
Masking tape
Fine permanent marker

Needlepoint yarns (see color key)
No. 20 tapestry needle
Six-strand grey cotton embroidery floss

Erica *To stitch a portrait of your very own home, lay tracing paper over a photo of your home and trace the outlines with a fine-tipped pen; enlarge the tracing to 6" x 10" or desired size, and working on graph paper to help you with the straight lines of the architectural details, simplify the outlines, to make an interesting and workable design.*
Transfer the design to canvas, and following your desired color scheme, complete steps 2 and 3 below. Cross-stitchers: Make this project on ½ yard of 14-mesh Aida cloth. Enlarge and transfer design; cross stitch large color areas, leaving white areas unworked fabric. Then embroider shingles on top of the cross stitch with cotton floss.

1. Enlarge the design onto squared paper (see p. 126). To transfer design to canvas, tape canvas on top of paper, aligning threads of canvas with straight lines of house; trace design outline onto canvas with permanent marker.

2. Following the design diagram, working in tent stitch (continental stitch—see p. 122), fill in needlepoint colors.

3. Embroider details on top of needlepoint (see p. 119): Use single strand of grey floss for shingles; work straight stitches, brick fashion; add a single dark grey backstitch line to define the lower edge of the roof. Block and mount needlepoint (see p. 119).

SWAN PILLOW
(Photo on p. 51)

Finished design size: 18 ½" x
   16 ½" including 1 ½" border
7-mesh needlepoint canvas,
   22 ½" x 20 ½"
Pencil
Bold black marker
Fine-tipped permanent marker
No. 16 tapestry needle
Persian yarn (see color key)
Lavender velvet (for backing)

*Erica To make a rug like the one
on page 32, use the same technique to
trace and stitch animals and birds in
four or more canvas squares; join
squares; surround with bargello border.*

1. Fold and crease canvas in half
and half again to establish center.
With pencil, mark horizontal and
vertical center lines. Enlarge pillow design to 15 ½" x 13 ½" and
outline with bold black marker;
place below canvas and trace
design onto canvas with permanent marker (see p. 126).

2. To outline border on canvas,
find center of design; measure
out from center 7 ¾" horizontally
and 6 ¾" vertically; draw rectangle all around by sliding pencil
between threads of canvas.

Repeat to add a second rectangle 1 ½" outside the first.

3. Using six strands of wool and
following color chart, stitch border
first, working in blocks of bargello
or brick stitch over four threads of
canvas (see p. 122 for stitches).
Next, work background, continuing in bargello or brick stitch and
blending wool colors as indicated
on chart.

4. When background is complete, using three strands of wool
work swan in crewel stitches, following color chart and working
into canvas as though it was
embroidery fabric, disregarding
mesh. Work wing feathers in horizontal long and short stitch, shading from pale to medium grey.
Work neck and body in split
stitch, following contours. Work

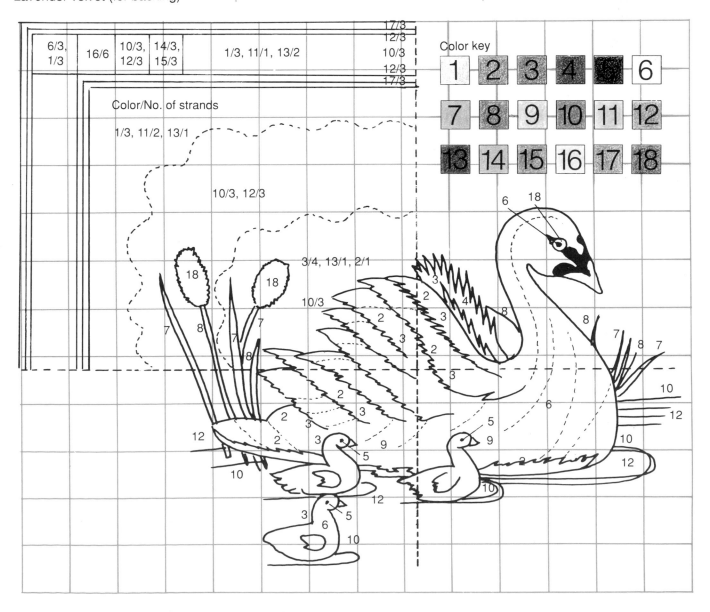

CREWEL ROSES

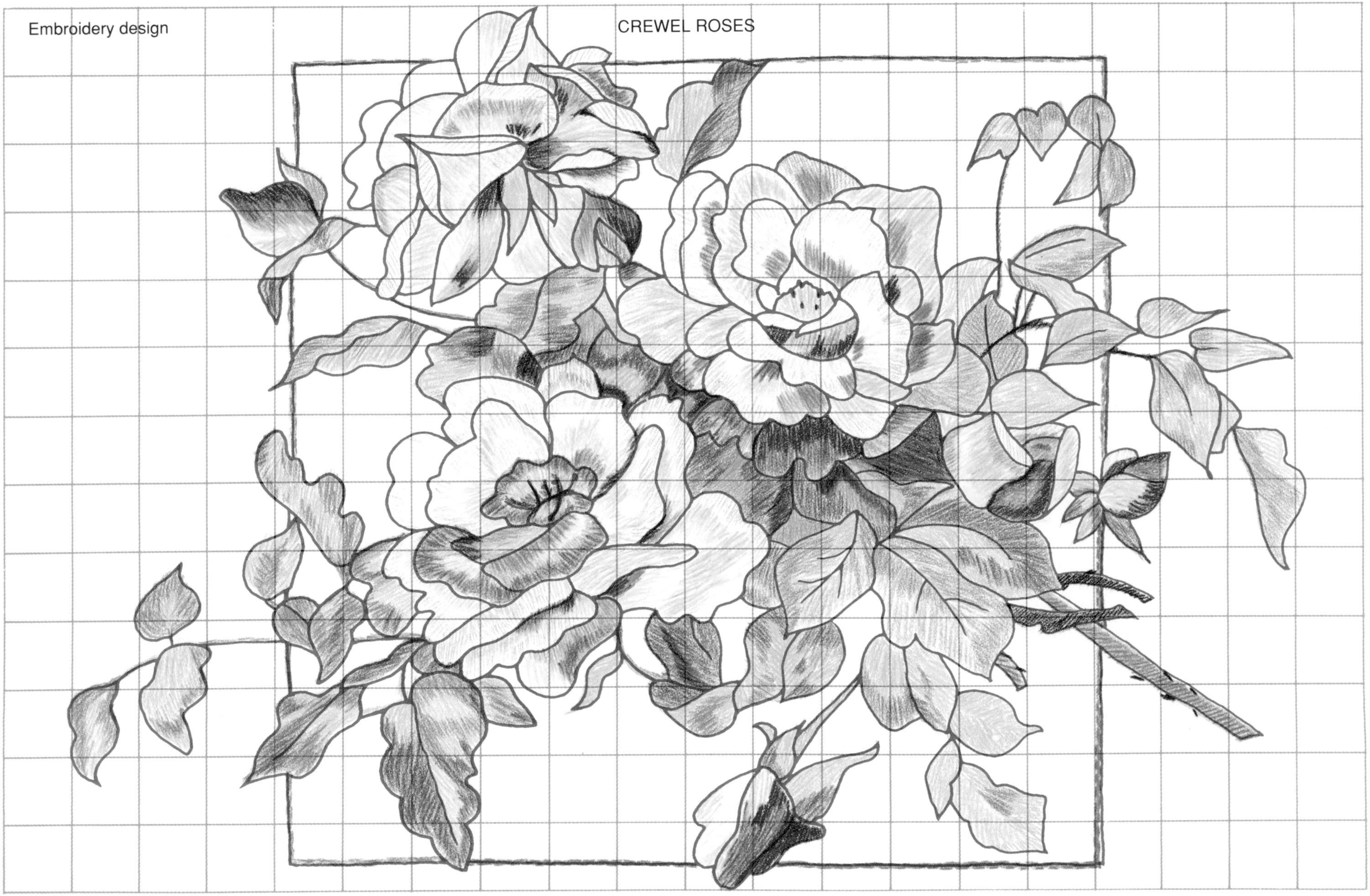

Color key

1 2 3 4 5 6 7 8 9 10 11 12 13 14 15 16 17 18 19 20 21

beak and eye in padded satin stitch.

5. Work cygnets in same manner as swan, with french-knot eyes and grey stem stitch outlining neck and wings. With two strands of wool, use clipped turkey work for bulrush with stem-stitch leaves. With one strand of wool, stitch lavender and pink water ripples on top of background.

6. Using three strands of wool, outline border with slanting gobelin stitch in medium pink bordered by khaki and lavender stem stitch, one row on either side. Block and mount pillow with lavender velvet backing (see p. 123). No piping or boxing is required.

CREWEL ROSES
(Photo on p. 52)

Finished size: 14" x 18" (actual design is 9" x 9")
Linen, wheat or other neutral color
Three-ply persian-type crewel yarn (see color key)
Six-strand ivory cotton embroidery floss
Embroidery frame or artist's stretcher strips
No. 4 crewel needle or No. 20 chenille needle for wool
No. 8 crewel needle for floss

1. Enlarge design and transfer to center of fabric (see p. 126). Following chart and photo for color placement, begin piece with rose to left of center at upper right petal. Using No. 4 crewel needle or No. 20 chenille needle and one strand of wool, work petals in long and short stitch, one color area at a time (see p. 119 for stitches). With No. 8 crewel needle and two strands of ivory floss, in long and short stitch work highlights right over and into ivory wool stitches, feathering stitches to blend in.

Erica The design pictured was worked on wheat-colored linen, but would be equally nice on a cream or black background fabric. Work from the outside edge of each flower towards the center. The petals and leaves are worked in bands of satin stitch. When you begin a new color, split the ends of the stitches of the previous color, coming up through the stitch from underneath. When you start a new petal, do not split the stitch, but work into the same hole as the previous stitch, to define the petal edge.

2. Using wool, satin stitch center of each rose, then add topstitched details: Work a few straight stitches and french knots in accent colors. Put finishing touches on the roses with additional topstitched accents.

3. Stitch buds in wool and then add floss highlights in same order of working as roses. Next, work leaves in satin stitch, beginning at outside of leaf and working towards stem; as with rose petals, overlap color areas within leaf by splitting ends of stitches of previous color. Complete leaves with topstitched details.

4. Using wool, with satin stitch and stem stitch, embroider stems. To complete the design, embroider the square outline with wool, using stem stitch.

VICTORIAN ROSES RUG
(Photo on p. 53)

5-mesh canvas, desired number of 26" x 26" squares
Paper and Trace Erase™ pen or permanent marker (optional)
No. 13 tapestry needle
Rug wool (see color key)
Coarsely textured linen or rug backing

Erica When selecting your canvas, be sure to allow at least 2" of extra canvas on all sides to allow for blocking and mounting. When choosing yarn, buy enough to complete your project so that the dye lots match.

The rug pictured was worked on 5-mesh canvas with rug wool, and each square measures 22" x 22". The design can be equally effective worked on a smaller canvas with finer wool. Each square is 114 stitches by 114 stitches. To find the finished size using a smaller canvas, divide 114 (the number of stitches) by size of canvas (mesh or stitches per inch). For example, if you choose a 10-mesh canvas, divide 114 by 10--the finished square will measure approximately 11" x 11".

Because each of the four roses is worked in four or five shades of one color, you can rotate the colors, making the deep red rose of one design pale pink in the next, and so on, giving each square of the rug a completely different look, yet keeping an overall balance. Alternatively, you can work the entire rug in shades of one color. Use a coarse rug backing; a close-textured backing will trap dirt inside the rug, and dirt cuts the stitches.

1. To count design from graph, find center of canvas by folding in half and half again. Center of graph is noted by an arrow. Begin stitching at this point. If you prefer to have your pattern directly on canvas, enlarge rose design (see p. 126) and center under canvas; using permanent marker or Trace Erase™ pen, trace design onto each canvas square. Follow graph for shading flowers and working geometric border.

2. Sort wool colors by flower; this makes it easy to rotate colors. Working in tent stitch (continental stitch--see p. 122), fill in flowers first, then leaves. Carefully count out and work border; finally work background.

3. When all pieces are complete, block each carefully--it is essential that they be square to enable you to make neat joins. Machine- or hand-seam squares together into strips; join strips to form rug. Open seams and press flat; line rug with backing fabric.

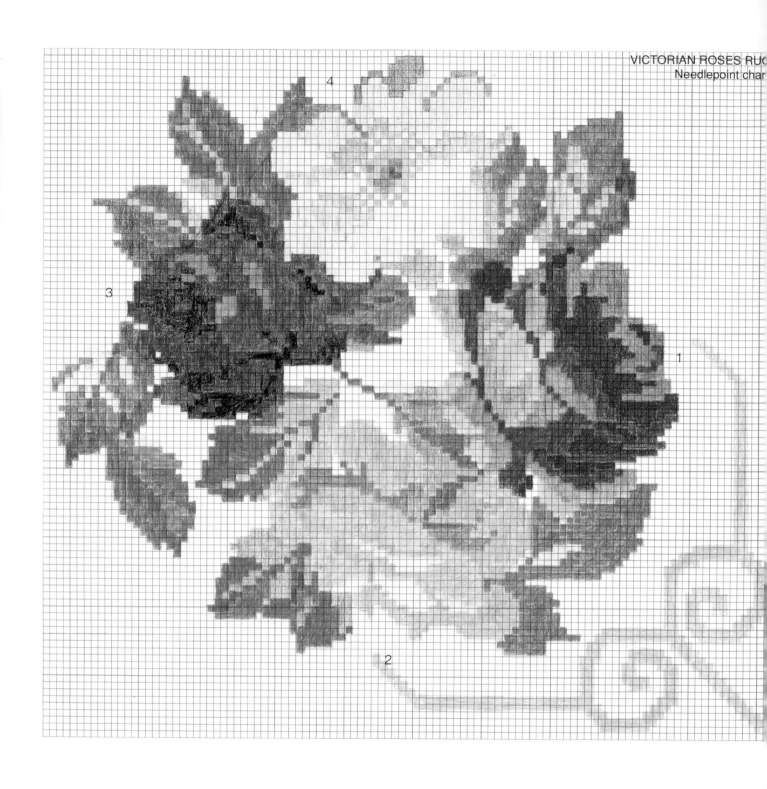

Color key   1. Pink rose   2. Yellow rose   3. Red rose   4. White rose   Leaves

Numbers
indicate
shadings
light to
dark.

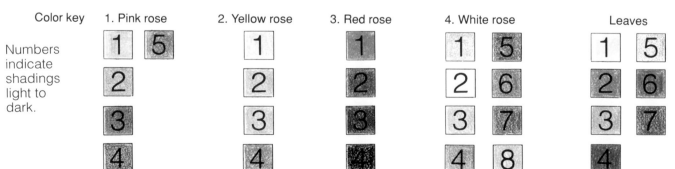

MINIATURE SALTBOX HOUSES
(Photo on p. 54)

Postcard-weight cardboard
White cotton broadcloth
Hard pencil
4 artist's stretcher strips
Staplegun or tacks
Grey fabric paint and brush
Gold metallic thread (lurex)
White glue or rubber cement
Six-strand cotton embroidery floss
Embroidery needle
Cotton balls

1. Enlarge house pattern pieces (see p. 126) and cut out in cardboard; cut out square openings for windows. With hard pencil, outline houses on fabric. Mount fabric in stretcher strips and secure with staples or tacks. With fabric paint on dry brush (no water), fill in outlines of house sections on fabric leaving inside of windows unpainted; refer to photo for colors. With gold thread, stitch shingles on roof using an open buttonhole stitch; embroider windows and door in laid work tied with cross bars (see p. 119 for stitches).

2. Cut out houses with ⅜" turnbacks all around; glue to cardboard with rubber cement or white glue, placing windows over openings in cardboard. Clean-finish edges of each piece. Join house sections by oversewing right sides together. Glue a cotton ball to each chimney opening; tape a tiny Christmas-tree light at lower edge of each house front so light glows through windows but cannot burn fabric.

PINE NEEDLE ORNAMENTS
(Photo on p. 56)

Finished size: about 2 ½" x 2 ½"
Per ornament:
   14-mesh Aida cloth, 2 ½" x 2 ½" piece
   Six-strand cotton embroidery floss (see color key)
   Red velvet
   ⅝"-wide pre-gathered lace,14" length
   ⅛"-wide Offray red satin ribbon, 6" length
   Calico, red, white and green print, 3" x 5" piece
   Muslin, 2 ½" x 6" piece

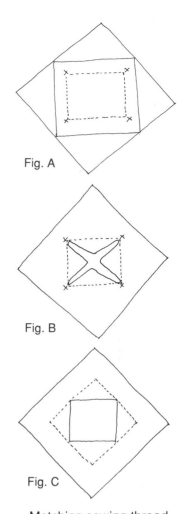

Fig. A

Fig. B

Fig. C

Matching sewing thread
Pine needles or potpourri

1. Find center of chart; find center of Aida cloth. With two strands of floss, stitch designs (see p. 119): Cross stitch wreath with green and bow with red; backstitch current year;scatter red french-knot berries over wreath.

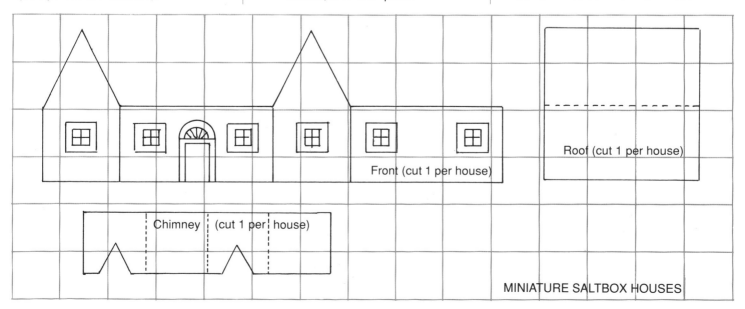

Front (cut 1 per house)

Roof (cut 1 per house)

Chimney (cut 1 per house)

MINIATURE SALTBOX HOUSES

Backstitch pine cone and branch with brown and current year with red; straight stitch green pine needles and randomly scatter red french-knot berries along branch.

2. Cut red velvet diamond large enough to lay stitched square on top diagonally (see fig. A). With right sides up, place four pins through both layers ½" from corners of stitched square; make tailor's tacks on velvet at these points; remove stitched square. Slash velvet diagonally between tacks to make four triangular flaps (fig. B). Right side up, fold four flaps underneath and press (fig. C). Lay velvet on top of stitched square with stitching showing through opening; handsew edges of opening securely to Aida cloth.

3. To make pillow back, cut calico in half to make two 3" x 2 ½" pieces. Narrow-hem long edge of one piece; with right sides out, baste pieces together at sides. With right side of hemmed calico piece facing right side of stitched front, stitch pillow back and front together without catching the hemmed calico edge, securing lace and ribbon loop in stitching and leaving an opening for turning. Clip corners; turn right side out; slipstitch opening closed.

4. To make stuffing sack, fold muslin in half crosswise, right sides together; stitch 3" sides together. Turn right side out and press top edge under ¼". Fill with pine needles or potpourri; slipstitch sack closed; insert into pillow back; tack opening closed.

CHRISTMAS RIBBON GLOBES
(Photo on p. 57)

Round balloons in various sizes
Ribbon, various colors, patterns
    and widths
Rubber gloves

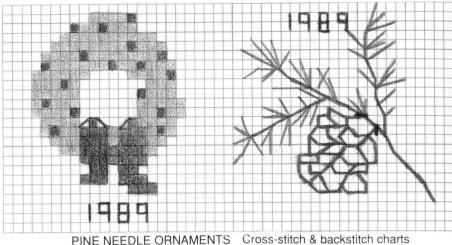

PINE NEEDLE ORNAMENTS   Cross-stitch & backstitch charts

Color key

Sponge
White glue
Clear spray-on fabric stiffener
Florist's wire

1. Blow up balloons: Smaller ones are for top of tree, larger are for base of tree. Working with rubber gloves, sponge and white glue, mix solution of equal parts glue and water. Cut lengths of ribbon to encircle balloon from top to bottom; coat with solution. Arrange ribbons vertically around balloons, securing ends at top with a knot or bow, or with a twist of florist's wire. Allow to dry overnight. Spray with clear fabric stiffener; when stiffener is dry, pop balloon; it will disappear inside globe.

VALENTINE BUNNY HEART
(Photo on p. 58)

14-mesh Aida cloth, ½ yard
Six-strand cotton embroidery floss
    (see color key)
Embroidery needle and frame
Trace Erase™ pen or hard pencil
Cotton or Aida cloth for backing

Eyelet trim, 1 ¼ yards
Matching sewing thread
Polyester fiberfill

1. Stretch fabric on frame (see p. 126). Find center of Aida cloth; mark with basting stitches. Count out lettering; use Trace Erase™ pen or hard pencil to draw each letter 7 stitches high on Aida cloth. Work cross stitch from center outward (see p. 119 for stitches). With single strand of black floss, topstitch finishing touches and outlines in backstitch and oblique backstitch. Wash and block embroidery (see p. 119).

VALENTINE BUNNY HEART

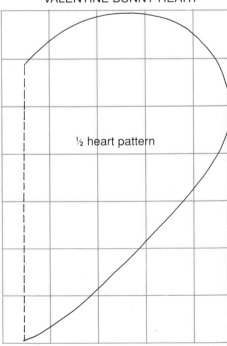

½ heart pattern

VALENTINE BUNNY HEART
Cross-stitch & backstitch chart

2. Enlarge heart pattern (see p. 126) to enclose design with at least ½" all around for seam allowance; make paper pattern. Pin paper pattern over stitchery and cut out. Use same pattern to cut out backing. Trim and mount pillow (see p. 123).

Erica *Experienced needleworkers know that in cross stitch it is easier and neater to bring the needle up in an empty space and down in a used space. To do this with the bunny heart, work down from the center, then turn both work and chart upside down and work the other half down from the center.*

Color key

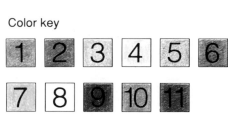

DUCK BUN-WARMER

(Photo on p. 59)

44"-wide muslin, ¾ yard
Calico, ½ yard yellow
Scrap of colorfast yellow felt
Scraps of batting
Polyester fiberfill or foam rubber
Buckram or canvas
Two ½" black buttons
Six-strand white cotton embroidery floss

1. Enlarge pattern pieces to desired size (see p. 126). Adding ½" seams all around, from muslin cut one pair each of duck sides and tail, two pairs wings and one duck bottom. From lining fabric, cut one pair of lining sides and one lining bottom. From yellow felt cut one beak (you may substitute lining fabric for felt).

2. Right sides together, seam duck sides at neck and head, from point C to point A, and at tail from point B to point D. Seam sides to bottom, matching points A and B on side to same points on bottom. Turn right side out. Stuff head, neck and chest with polyester fiberfill.

3. Baste batting to back of each lining piece. Seam lining bottom to curved edge of each lining side, matching points E and F.

4. Using pattern for lining bottom, cut one piece from buckram or canvas and two pieces from batting. Baste together with both batting pieces on top of buckram; place in bottom of duck, batting side up; tack in place. Place lining on top of batting inside duck; turn over top edges of duck and lining; slipstitch.

5. Baste batting to back of one tail piece (other tail piece forms facing) and two wing pieces. Muslin sides together, seam tail to facing, leaving opening for turning. Trim batting close to stitch-ing; turn right side out. Turn in open edges and slipstitch. Topstitch tail along broken lines. With embroidery floss, scatter french knots (see p. 119) if desired. Make wings in same manner as tail; embellish with embroidered feather stitch.. Tack tail to duck, matching center back. Pin wings to duck at X's, so they can swing upwards to cover buns; tack in place.

6. Fold beak in half, matching the two curves; whipstitch (or seam, if fabric) curved edges. Slide beak over duck with seam downward. Slipstitch straight edge (turning under first, if fabric) to duck. Affix buttons for eyes.

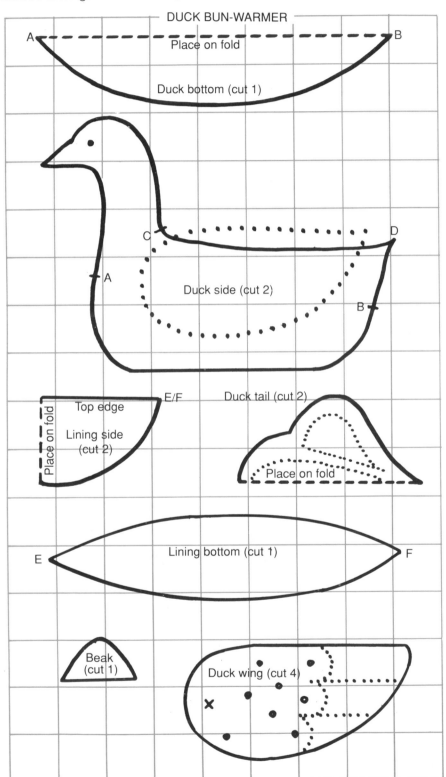

DUCK BUN-WARMER

A — Place on fold — B
Duck bottom (cut 1)

C — D
Duck side (cut 2)
A
B

E/F — Duck tail (cut 2)
Place on fold
Top edge
Lining side (cut 2)
Place on fold

E — Lining bottom (cut 1) — F

Beak (cut 1)

Duck wing (cut 4)

KNITTED KITTENS
(Photo on p. 59)

Size: Directions are given for size small (4 ½" high). Changes for medium (5 ½") and large (8") are in parentheses.
Lion Brand Molaine or any yarn to obtain correct gauge, two 40g balls beige
Knitting needles, one pair size 7 or size to obtain correct gauge
Polyester fiberfill
Scraps of felt
White and black sewing thread
3 checked bows
Small basket
GAUGE: 18 sts and 20 rows = 4" (10 cm) in St st. To save time, take time to check gauge.
ABBREVIATIONS USED:
  beg = beginning
  dec = decrease
  inc = increase
  k = knit
  p = purl
  st = stitch
  St st = Stockinette
    stitch (K 1 row, p 1 row)
See knitting basics on p. 122.

Body back/front

½ front paw

½ ear

Tail

½ hind leg

KNITTED KITTENS

Erica *Be sure to test your gauge by first knitting a practice swatch. Change needle sizes if necessary to obtain correct gauge. Make one kitten in each size, then place in basket.*

1. Body back: Beg at lower edge, cast on 13 (17, 26) sts. Work in St st for 12 (13,14) rows; dec one st each end of next row–11(15, 24) sts. Work even for 3 (9, 3) rows; dec one st each end of next row–9 (13, 22) sts. Work even for 2 (4, 3) rows; dec one st each end of next row–7 (11, 20) sts. Medium size only: Bind off all sts. Work even for 1 (0,3) rows. Small size only: Bind off all sts. Large size only: Dec one st each end of next row–18 sts. Work even for 4 rows; dec one st each end of next row–16 sts. Work even for 3 rows; dec 1 st each end of next row–14 sts. Work even for 5 rows. Bind off.

2. Body front: Work same as for back. Sew side seams, leaving bottom and top open. Bottom section : Beg at one end, cast on 11 (17,16) sts. Work even in St st for 9 (10,18) rows; bind off.

3. Ear (make two): For first half, beg at bottom of ear, cast on 6 (6, 7) sts. Work even in St st for 4 (5, 7) rows; dec one st each end of next row–4 (4, 5) sts. Work even for 1 (1, 1) row; dec one st each end of next row–2 (2, 3) sts. Small size only: Bind off all sts. Medium and large size: Work even for 0 (1, 2) rows. Bind off all sts. Second half: Work same as first half. Sew ear halves together at side seams, leaving bottom open; stuff lightly. Insert ears into top opening of body, gathering bottom of ear slightly; sew seam closed. Stuff body and sew bottom section of body in place.

4. Front paw (make two): For first half, beg at base of paw, cast on 6 (7, 9) sts. Work even in St st for 8, (9,11) rows; bind off. Second half: Work same as first half. Sew paw halves together, rounding corners and leaving one side open; stuff paws and sew seams closed. Sew to lower front body.

5. Hind leg (make two): For first half, beg at bottom of leg, cast on 10 (14,18) sts. Work even in St st

for 6 (8,10) rows. Bind off 5 (8,8) sts at beg of next row–5 (6,10) sts. Work even for 5 (7,9) rows; bind off. Second half: Work same as first half, reversing shaping. Sew and stuff, then join to either side of body.

6. Tail: Beg at base of tail, cast on 11 (13,17) sts. Work even in St st for 6 (8, 8) rows; *dec one st each end of next row. Work even for 3 (4, 3) rows.* Rep from * to * 1 (1, 2) times more—7 (9,11) sts. Dec 1 st each end of next row—5 (7, 9) sts. Work even for 3 (1, 4) rows. Small and medium size only: Bind off all sts. Large size only: Dec 1 st each end of next row—7 sts. Work even for 2 rows; bind off all sts. Fold tail in half lengthwise; sew seam, leaving opening at base of tail. Stuff and sew to lower back body. If desired, brush knitting to fluff.

7. Features: For each eye, cut one circle each about ¼" (⅜", ½") diameter from white, light blue and black felt; sew in position on face. For nose: Cut one ¼" (½",½") triangle from black felt; sew in position. Embroider mouth with black thread and whiskers with white thread; pull through strands of thread at either side of mouth area. Tack on fabric bow.

APPLIQUÉD SHORTS
(Photo on p. 61)

Purchased shorts
Scraps of cotton fabric
Six-strand cotton embroidery floss in assorted colors
Crewel needle
Curved scissors

1. Make freehand sketches, xeroxes and tracings of all his favorite things, using photos, cartoons, etc.,for reference. Simple silhouette shapes will be the most effective and are easiest to handle. With curved scissors, cut out

shapes in appropriate fabrics; arrange them in a pleasing design on the shorts.

2. Snip curves so turnbacks will be smooth and flat; baste, and apply.to shorts with tiny invisible hemming stitches. If you have any complicated scenes with overlapping motifs, assemble these separately, stitching down on fine muslin; then cut out whole area and apply to shorts in one piece (see p. 119 for appliqué).

3. Using two or three strands of embroidery floss (or thickness desired), embroider around shapes with outline stitches such as stem, chain or backstitch to finish the applique neatly (see p. 119 for stitches). Add accents of satin stitch, french knots and fishbone stitch, working right through all layers. As a final embellishment, add amusing three-dimensional details such as feathers, beads, buttons, tufts of wool, etc., to make the shorts a real conversation piece.

PATCHWORK PICNIC BLANKET
(Photo on p. 60)

100% cotton calico, gingham or
   broadcloth
Graph paper
Brown paper (for hand-patched
   blanket)
Trace Erase™ pen or hard pencil
   (for machine-patched blanket)
Non-slip sandpaper, see-through
   acetate, lightweight cardboard
   or pre-made metal templates
Cotton sewing thread
Backing fabric
Quilt batting and binding
Quilting hoop or frame
Quilting thread and needle

1. To make templates, cut 2" x 2" squares of graph paper; glue to template material and cut out squares same size (or use pre-made metal templates).

2. To patch by hand: Use templates to trace precisely equal-size squares onto brown paper; cut out and use as paper pattern. Lay paper pattern pieces on straight of fabric, spacing apart to allow for ⅜" turnbacks; baste each in position with a single stitch in the center. Cut out fabric squares adding ⅜" turnbacks all around. Carefully press, then baste turnbacks over paper pattern edges (fig. A), stacking squares to ensure they are same size (if your pressing is very accurate, you may eliminate the basting). Right sides together, oversew squares to join (fig. B) in diagonal stripe arrangement as described in step 4.

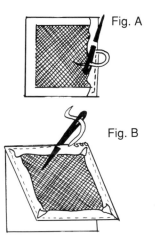

Fig. A

Fig. B

Fig. C

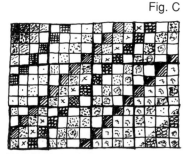

PATCHWORK PICNIC BLANKET

3. To patch by machine: Place templates on straight of fabric, spacing apart to allow for ⅜" turnbacks; draw around templates directly onto fabric with Trace Erase™ pen or hard pencil. Cut out fabric with ⅜" turnbacks all around. Right sides together, machine-stitch squares to join in diagonal stripe arrangement as described in step 4.

4. Arranging colors in diagonal bands of light and dark hues (see

color photo and fig. C), join two pairs of squares separately; join pairs to make large block of four squares; repeat to make four large blocks of four squares each; join to make one large block of 16 squares. Repeat to make several blocks of 16 squares; join blocks in strips to obtain desired length; join more strips to obtain desired width.

5. Sandwich and baste together quilt top, batting and backing. Insert into quilting hoop and hand- or machine-quilt layers together as desired, using running stitches (see p. 123). Finish edges with quilt binding.

TRAPUNTO PILLOW
(Photo on p. 62)

Finished size: 20" x 20", including
   border
Muslin
Sharp scissors
Six-strand peach cotton embroi-
   dery floss
Embroidery frame and needle
Loose batting
Down, fiberfill or pillow form

1. Use ½" seam allowances throughout. Cut three 21" x 21" squares of muslin. Set one piece aside for quilt backing; finish other two pieces as quilt top and pillow backing (see p. 123) but do not assemble pillow.

2. Enlarge harvest basket design to fit in 15" x 15" center of pillow (see p. 126); transfer to one muslin square.With quilt basting stitch, baste second square of muslin to reverse side.

3. With design uppermost, mount the basted fabric into an embroidery hoop (see p. 126). Using three strands of embroidery floss, outline design with stem stitch (see p. 119). Working stem stitch from reverse side results in backstitch on right side, and working

from the back prevents design lines from showing on the front.

4. When stitching is complete, remove basting threads. Separate quilt backing from top with two crossed pins; insert point of scissors into muslin above pins (pins help prevent cutting into top fabric); carefully cut slits in backing and push loose batting between layers with tips of scissors, padding work lightly but firmly. Do not pack so tightly that work becomes hard and rigid, but make sure batting is pushed in evenly to all corners and narrow areas. Securely sew up slits.

5. To mount pillow with flange or flat band border, sew seams with right sides facing 2" beyond established pillow edge; leave half of one edge open for stuffing. Open seams with warm iron; reverse, turn right side out; press flat again. Sew seam around pillow 2" from edge, again leaving opening for stuffing. Insert pillow; sew openings closed. Make twisted cord of embroidery floss (see fig. A); stitch cord over inner seam, looping corners.

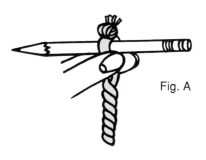

Fig. A

ANNIVERSARY SAMPLER
(Photo on p. 63)

Finished size: 14" x 14"
14-mesh mono needlepoint canvas
Artist's stretcher strips
Thumbtacks or staplegun
White candlewick floss
Tapestry needle

TRAPUNTO PILLOW
Quilting design

Erica As you work, smooth out threads to lie flat and even. Since much canvas is left unworked, be careful not to carry thread along back of work as it may show in front.

1. Find center of canvas by folding canvas in half and half again. Mark center lines with white basting thread. Enlarge and transfer design to canvas (see p. 126), filling in correct year and initials from the alphabet and numbers on next page; stretch canvas on stretcher strip frame with tacks or staplegun (see p. 126).

2. Thread needle with four strands of floss and begin by working central part of design. Working in vertical satin stitch (fig. A), come up on one side of printed shape and down on other side, filling in shapes and covering outlines.

3. Work entire design as described in step 2, except the following areas . Work bird's tail in vertical brick stitch (fig. B),bird's wings in horizontal bands of satin stitch over one thread of canvas, the man's cravat in brick stitch following neckline over one thread of canvas and lady's skirt and man's jacket base in cross stitch (fig. C) over two threads of canvas. Leave open canvas in center of all flowers and in set of leaves above man's and lady's heads.

4. Before stitching lace border, baste a line marking square around design to establish position. Following cross-stitch border chart for Wildflower & Lace pillow on p. 74, stitch the bold areas using three strands of floss, working first the inner and then the outer border; then fill in light areas using a single strand. Block and mount needlepoint as a picture or pillow (see p. 119).

ANNIVERSARY SAMPLER

Central design

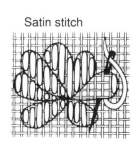

Cross stitch

Satin stitch

Brick stitch

Cross-stitch alphabet and numbers

Purchased photo album with
   photo frame cover
2"-wide flat lace banding, 2 yards
1"-wide ruffled lace edging, 1 yard
½" wide ruffled lace edging, ½ yard
Flat gold ribbon, 1 yard
⅜"-wide Offray double-faced
   satin ribbon, 12 yards
Fabric glue and masking tape
Florist's leaves (optional)

1. To make outer lace border, lay
2"-wide flat lace banding wrong
side up across lower edge of
album, holding in place with
masking tape. Fold up corner of
lace diagonally; run lace along
right edge of album; tape in
place. Work around entire edge
in this way to form flat lace border
with four corners of standing vertical pleats. Pin and baste pleats;
untape lace frame from album
and invisibly stitch pleats.

2. If lace is thin, fold pleat flat on
top of seam; turn over and glue
lace to album. If lace is thick,
stitch, then trim turnbacks; press
flat; open and glue in place with
seams down. To make inner lace
border, repeat steps 1 and 2 to
form a second lace frame inside
the first.

3. Glue edge of wider lace ruffle
around outer edge of central
photo frame; glue edge of nar-
rower ruffle around inner edge.
Tape gold ribbon into position to
form border on flat lace as in
color photo; tie attractive bow at
lower edge; untape and glue in
place.

4. With double-faced satin ribbon make twelve ribbon roses
(see p. 124). Referring to photo,
position and glue three roses in
each corner. If desired, add
florist's leaves.

Alphabet of Techniques and Stitches

APPLIQUÉ

Appliqué is the technique of stitching one fabric to another. The applied shapes should lie flat and smooth without bubbles or wrinkles; in fact, the two materials should become as one. This is most easily accomplished if you follow three important guidelines: Work in an embroidery frame; select 100% cotton fabrics so that turnbacks will be easy to handle and not spring back and behave badly; and always cut fabrics so that grain of appliquéd piece will run in same direction as grain of background fabric once stitched together.

1. Begin by marking outlines of shapes on appliqué fabric. Position shapes on fabric at exactly the same angle they will ultimately be when applied to background fabric (in this way, the two fabrics will have the same "pull").

2. To appliqué by hand, cut out each shape, leaving ¼" turnbacks. Outline each shape with staystitching ¼" from edge. Clip curves, turn, press and baste turnbacks to wrong side of fabric. Pin each piece in position on background fabric; sew down with tiny stitches made at right angles to edges. With small shapes, it may be easier to pin them in position without first preparing turnbacks, then fold under turnbacks with needle to make a smooth clear outline, stitching down as you go.

3. To appliqué by machine, draw design on square of fabric and lay it on background fabric right sides up, matching grains. Outline with straight machine stitching, then cut away excess fabric around design. Outline with satin stitch (or use overlock stitch on serger machine); trim loose ends.

BLOCKING EMBROIDERY OR NEEDLEPOINT

Before blocking any article, test a corner of the work to make sure that both thread and background fabric are colorfast. If not, you must have work blocked by professional dry cleaning. You will need your untrimmed finished work, mild soap and water, a setcher strip frame (p. 126), an old sheet, a heavy-duty staplegun or carpet tacks and a hammer; pliers, a right-angle rule, a cloth and a cardboard tube.

1. If your needlework needs cleaning, soak it in cold water in the bathtub before blocking and wash gently with a mild soap (test the soap first to make sure it won't bleed the colors). If the work does not need cleaning, size it while dry, as directed below, and wet

afterward; it will be easier to handle.

2. Lay work out on a board or old table which has first been covered with a sheet. Crewel and crewel point should be blocked face upward to allow the raised stitches to stand out. Needlepoint should always be placed face downward for a smooth effect. Needlepoint needs special attention in blocking because sometimes the stitches pull the design out of shape.

3. With carpet tacks (not thumbtacks, which are not strong enough) or staplegun, fasten work to frame, securing the four corners first, measuring opposite sides to see that they are even and making sure corners are true right angles. Use the two sides of the frame or table to guide you by placing the first two sides of the design close to the edges. Pull the design out firmly with pliers to make sure it is really taut.

4. Don't worry if tacks stain the canvas with rust marks—this will be cut away with the turning (the extra canvas that disappears in the seams). Add four more tacks or staples, one in the center of each side, then eight more tacks in the spaces between. Continue until tacks or staples are about ¼" apart.

5. Take a cloth and a bowl of water and thoroughly soak the needlework, then allow it to dry in its own time, away from direct sunlight and heat. When thoroughly dry, take it up, and if it is not being mounted immediately, roll it loosely around a cardboard tube, right side outward so that the stitches are not crushed against one another.

CREWEL/CREWEL POINT STITCHES

Backstitch

Bullion knot

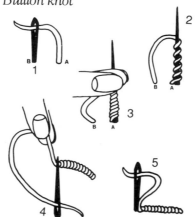

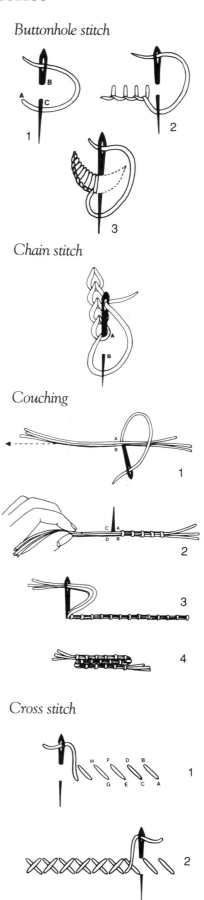

Buttonhole stitch

Chain stitch

Couching

Cross stitch

Feather stitch, broad

Feather stitch, straight

Feather stitch, zigzag

Fishbone stitch

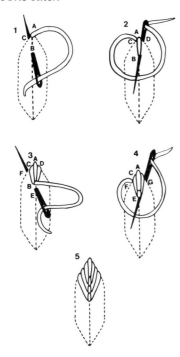

Fly stitch

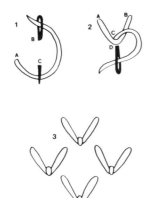

French knot

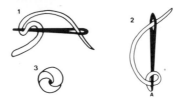

French knots on long stitch

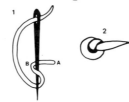

Gobelin stitch

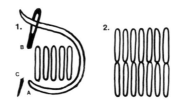

Gobelin stitch, slanting

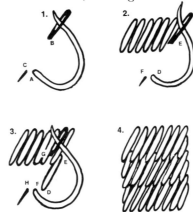

Gobelin stitches are worked on canvas only, for crewel point or needlepoint.

Herringbone stitch

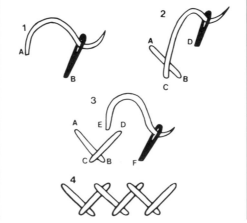

Herringbone stitch, close (for shadow work)

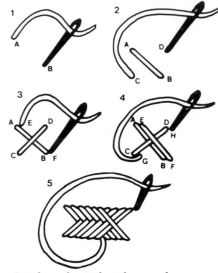

Laid work, tied with cross bars

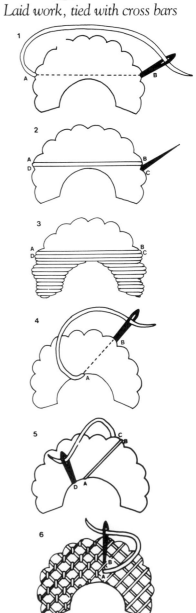

Laid work, tied diagonally

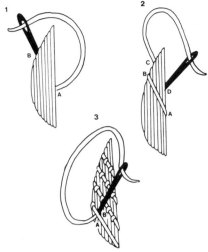

Lazy daisy stitch (detached chain stitch)

Long and short stitch

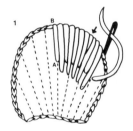

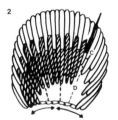

Satin stitch

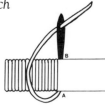

Satin stitch, padded

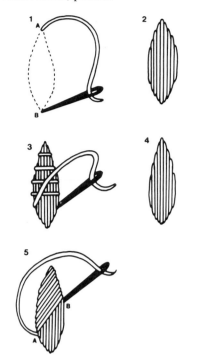

Satin stitch, slanting

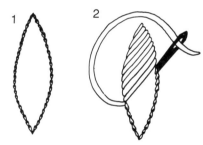

Split stitch

Stem stitch

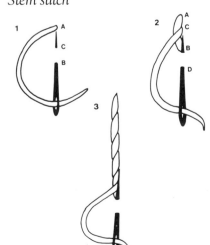

Stem stitch, raised

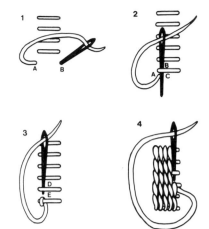

Straight stitch

Turkey work, cut and uncut

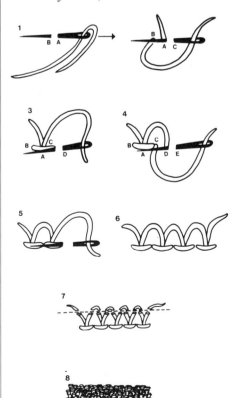

121

KNITTING

Knit stitch

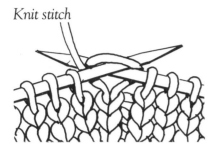

Purl stitch

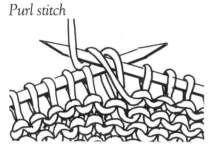

Increase (k in front and back of st)

Decrease (k 2 tog)

Casting on

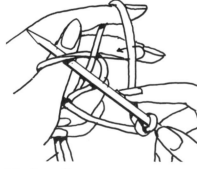

Binding off

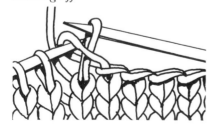

NEEDLEPOINT

In needlepoint you work over the threads of the mesh or canvas—a surface covering. Your needlepoint stitches are bound by the weave of the fabric and can only go vertically, horizontally or diagonally.

Starting and ending off

1. Starting: Having knotted your thread, take the needle down through the canvas, 6 or 7 threads away from where you intend to begin stitching, leaving knot on top. Start stitching, working toward knot, covering long thread which lies on reverse side. When you have worked up to knot, cut it off—end of thread will be held securely under canvas by stitches.

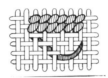

2. When finished with a thread, bring it to top of canvas some distance from last stitch. Leave thread there until, as with knot, long thread on back has been covered by more stitching. Cut off end of thread.

Bargello, flame

Bargello, random

Bargello, wave

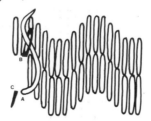

Plaid point

1. Using long enough thread to complete row, come up at top left corner of design. Following diagram, come up, count one thread down and one thread over to left, and go down. Come up, level with the first stitch, leaving one thread open between. Repeat across, skipping every other stitch. Check reverse side: If you have worked correctly you will have same pattern (stitches simply slant in opposite direction).

2. Now work another row next to first, placing stitches under spaces of first row. Because all stitches slant in same direction, several rows together will form diagonal line effect. Work three rows of first color, four rows of second, then three rows of first again.

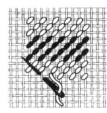 

3. Now work all vertical rows exactly the same as horizontal rows, using colors in same order. Verticals automatically fill in spaces left by skipped stitches on horizontal rows; when you have completed three rows of first color, four rows of second and three rows of first again, you will have a real plaid—alike on both sides. End off by weaving threads invisibly back into stitches at end of each row.

Tent stitch (continental stitch), horizontal rows

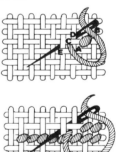

Tent stitch (continental stitch), vertical rows

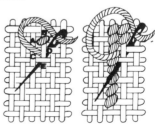

Tent stitch (continental stitch), diagonal lines

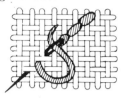

Tent stitch (continental stitch), diagonal rows

PILLOWS

Pillows may be made up with lace or eyelet embroidery edgings (such as the Invitation Pillow), with pipings (such as the Thanksgiving Trapunto Pillow) and/or with boxings, a narrow band of fabric mitered at the corners and stitched between back and front to give the pillow a box effect (such as the Stenciled Bed Pillow). When made up without a boxing or edging, pillows are referred to as knife-edged (such as the Scrap Art Pillows). In the instructions below, simply substitute boxing or whatever kind of edging you are using for the lace specified; the method will be the same. You will need: brown paper or tracing paper, muslin, polyester fiberfill or other stuffing, lace or other edging material, your finished pillow front and back and matching sewing thread.

1. If necessary, make a paper pattern for your pillow, adding ½" seam allowance beyond your finished size.

2. To make a pillow form (inner pillow), follow paper pattern and cut out two shapes from muslin for back and front. Stitch all around, leaving a 4" opening for turning. Turn right side out and fill with stuffing. Handstitch opening closed.

3. Gather lace, or make piping (to make piping, cover cord with strip of bias-cut fabric; stitch close to cord). Following paper pattern, cut out embroidered (or quilted or stitched) pillow front and pillow back. Place gathered lace in

position around border of embroidery, lining up edges with ruffle toward center so that there will be ¼" of lace in seam.

4. Sew lace in position, holding ruffle toward inside, right sides together. With right sides together, pin pillow back to front and ruffle. Stitch together front, back and ruffle, allowing ½" in seam and leaving a 4" opening for turning. Turn right side out and insert pillow form. Handstitch opening closed.

QUILTING

Soft fabrics are best for quilting, so that the finished quilt will be light and airy; among the best are cotton, Dacron, crepe de chine, fine muslins or batiste. Heavy fabrics flatten the batting or filling and reduce the warmth. Use waxed quilting thread for strength and quilting needles that are short and strong, making even stitching possible.

1. Baste the three layers of your quilt together. The broad quilt basting stitch is ideal for this; it holds all the fabrics together as though they were one (fig. A). Knot the thread, and starting at the top left, work down to the bottom of your quilt, taking a series of evenly spaced horizontal stitches. At the bottom, go back and form a cross stitch to secure the thread. Cover the entire area of your quilt in this way, spacing the rows about 2" apart.

2. Mount quilt into frame—square or oval if you are quilting entire top, round if you are doing apartment quilting (quilting each entire block before joining it to another block—see below). Do not stretch layers too tightly; leave quilt slightly slack in frame. Begin with a quilter's knot (fig. B) or bury a small knot in the batting by pulling thread until knot pops between layers (fig. C).

3. The quilting stitch is simply a running

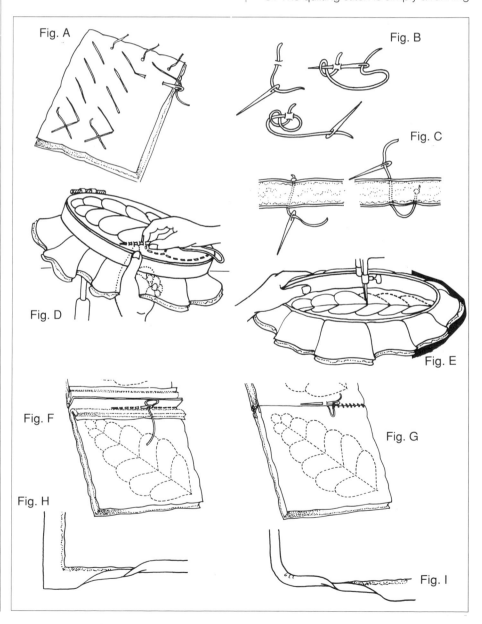

Fig. A

Fig. B

Fig. C

Fig. D

Fig. E

Fig. F

Fig. G

Fig. H

Fig. I

stitch. With one hand on top and other underneath, push needle straight down through all three layers, pricking finger underneath (just to make sure you are there); return needle to top (fig. D. Continue, taking as many stitches as you can get easily on needle. Each stitch length should be equal to space between stitches, and stitches should be of equal length on either side of quilt. Some quilters like to feel the needle as it comes through; others protect their fingers with a leather thimble or tape. Train yourself to use either hand on top; this makes it simpler to work in different directions. To end, knot thread, take last stitch and pop knot into batting. Run needle through batting a few inches before cutting thread.

4. If you are doing apartment quilting, leave 2" of fabric unquilted all around edge of block so that you can make neat joins afterwards. To quilt by machine, first stretch block with quilting design marked in a small round hoop. Remove presser foot. Thickness of hoop should be on top so that fabric can lie flat against base of sewing machine (fig. E). Joining can be done by first seaming right sides of blocks together (fig. F). Then blindstitch seams together on reverse side (fig. G).

5. One of the most popular ways to finish the edge of a quilt is to bring the lining over the top and blindstitch it around the edges for a narrow binding. Lining should always be cut larger than quilt top and batting in case you decide to use this easy finish (fig. H).

6. Bias binding is another excellent way of finishing the edges of a quilt. Since the edges receive the mmost wear, it is a good idea to double the bias fabric. Stitch to top of quilt, right sides facing; then turn it over and hemstitch it to lining, easing around corners (fig. I).

RIBBON EMBROIDERY

Keep needle as close to end of ribbon as possible; try to keep ribbon flat through eye of needle.

1. Insert needle halfway through fabric to begin stitch; gently push fabric threads aside to enlarge hole. Gently draw needle and ribbon through fabric, taking care not to twist the ribbon—this applies to stitches on both right and wrong sides of fabric.

2. Be sure ribbon lies flat on fabric or forms an even loop (as in lazy daisy stitch); ribbon must also lie flat on wrong side of fabric. As an alternative to knotting ribbon on wrong side, leave 2" ends when beginning and ending stitching; secure ends to other stitching with floss or sewing thread.

RIBBON ROSES
Pulled roses

You will need 1"-wide ribbon, ¾ yard per rose.

1. Fold length of ribbon exactly in half and mark the halfway point. Lay ribbon flat on table horizontally. Fold down and crease ribbon diagonally left of center so it lies vertically and at right angles to horizontal piece at right (fig. A). Fold and crease right-hand section of ribbon horizontally over vertical; the ribbon will be at right angles (fig. B). Now, fold vertical piece up over horizontal, again at right angles (fig. C). Continue folding and creasing ribbon sections alternately over previous fold with each strip at right angles to the one before (figs. D, E, F). This results in a stack of interlocking squares.

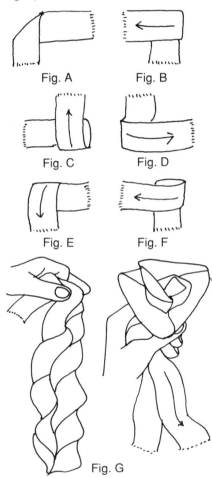

Fig. A   Fig. B

Fig. C   Fig. D

Fig. E   Fig. F

Fig. G

2. When all ribbon has been folded in this way, grasp the two projecting ends securely between fingers and thumb; allow folded ribbon to drop down like a twisted chain (fig. G). Hold one end of ribbon with one hand and at the same time pull up on the other end with your other hand; as you pull, ribbon bunches up, forming a rose. Stop pulling when you see the rose you like; stitch the two ends together. Voila!

Rolled roses

You will need double-faced satin ribbon, any width, ¾ yard per rose, and some florist's wire.

1. Lay ribbon horizontally on table. Fold right end of ribbon diagonally forward leaving a 2"–3" vertical tag (fig. A). Holding the ribbon firmly at right angles, roll short end of ribbon tightly, up to fold, forming a long, narrow tube (fig. B). Fold back ribbon at an angle, hold short end at right angle to rolled tube; roll again to fold (figs. C, D). Continue folding and rolling around rose in this manner until desired size (figs. E, F).

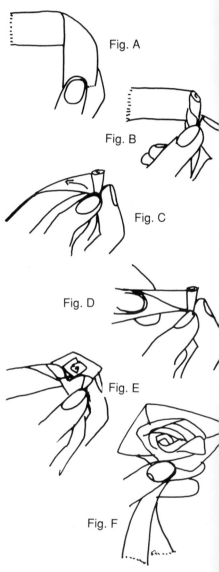

Fig. A

Fig. B

Fig. C

Fig. D

Fig. E

Fig. F

2. When complete, hold the two ends of ribbon together and wrap with florist's wire. To make a longer support, add some florist's wire as you begin the first roll. If the rose seems too high in the center, pull down on one of the ends of ribbon until it becomes smaller and lower. If the center of the rose is too low, pull it out with your finger and thumb to the desired height.

SEWING

French seam

1. With wrong sides together, pin or baste together two edges to be joined. Seam, ⅝" in from raw edges. Open seams, press flat; trim raw edges close. Press right sides together and seam ⅛" away from edge, by hand or machine with running stitches. The result will be a narrow hem finished neatly inside.

Hand-covered buttons

Buttons to cover may be bought in any notions or fabric store. Simply follow the manufacturer's easy instructions.

Point de Paris (pin stitch)

Use a large tapestry needle on organdy or fine lawn to open large holes; work with a strong, fine thread and pull each stitch firmly so the stitch appears to be a row of openwork holes, as an entre deux seam.

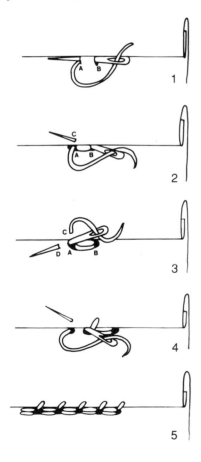

Entre deux seam

Entre deux is a narrow row of holes worked over a seam, similar to point de Paris or point turc. A machine-made version is available by the yard in fabric or notion stores. When stitched between the two edges to be joined, the result is a fine openwork row of holes instead of a seam.

Point turc (punch stitch)

This is like point de Paris, but produces a double instead of a single row of holes. Once you have mastered steps 1-9, pull each stitch tightly to open large holes in the fabric as in step 10. The stitches should be so tight that they almost disappear, the finished effect being formed by the holes.

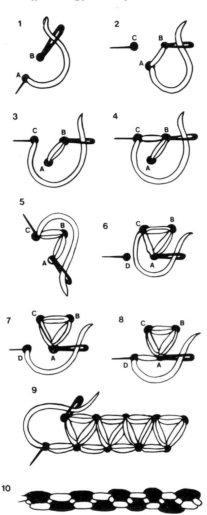

SMOCKING

Preparing fabric

1. Using iron-on dot transfer pattern: Lay transfer face down on wrong side of fabric area to be smocked; leave specified amount free for seams along side edges. Make sure rows of dots are lined up exactly with grain of fabric (if not exactly aligned, gathers will not set well and finished smocking will hang crookedly). Pin transfer in place; with a hot iron, press down until wax melts and transfer lifts up easily. (Lift and press iron only, as rubbing will cause transfer to smudge; take care not to burn fabric)). Using dot pattern as a guide for gathering threads, work across row with running stitches going in at one dot and out at the next.

2. Using Trace Erase™ tear-away interfacing grid: This product makes gathering easy without marking your fabric. Simply lay grid on top of wrong side of fabric area to be smocked; baste in place. Using grid as a guide for gathering threads, work across row with running stitches going in and out every two squares of the grid.

Gathering fabric

Gathering machines are available, but to gather by hand, work as follows.

1. Thread needle with more than enough contrasting-color thread to complete a line of gathers (it is impossible to start in the middle of a line, so you must not run short). At top right-hand edge, start with a knot and a backstitch; secure thread firmly. (There is nothing more annoying than to work a whole row of gathers, draw them up and then see them all pull out because the thread was not secured at the beginning of the row!) Work across each row with running stitches going in and out, guided by the dots or grid squares (or if you're working on an evenly printed fabric, such as gingham, just use the pattern of the fabric itself).

2. On the next row below, repeat exactly so that when fabric is drawn up, vertical folds form. (If your spots are too far apart and you fear the folds will be too deep if you go in at one spot, out at the next, then instead go in at one spot, out halfway to next spot, then in at next spot, etc.)

3. When all gathering threads are in place, lay fabric flat; pull up on threads in pairs until folds lie side by side. When you draw up gathers, threads should run through the middle of the fold (see fig. A). (If you do as many other books tell you, and pick up a small amount of fabric at each spot instead of going in and out, gathering threads will run along the surface instead of through the middle of the folds. This makes sleazy gathers, hard to control and keep even.) Folds should lie smoothly together like tubes, not too tight or loose.

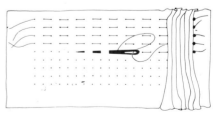

4. Secure gathers by twisting each pair of threads around a pin placed at edge of folds (see fig. B). This allows you to easily adjust folds, if necessary, after you begin stitching.

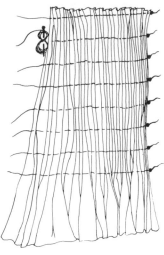

Fig. B

Steaming fabric

1. When smocking is complete, set gathers by steaming them with steam iron; after steaming, stitches will stand out clearly and reeds will be beautifully rounded. When fabric is completely dry, remove gathering threads.

Cable stitch, single and double

With each stitch, thread is held alternately above or below needle.

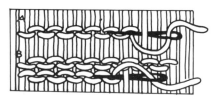

Chevron stitch

This is one of the most versatile stitches: Good for the focal point of a band of smocking, and the basic stitch used in "picture" smocking. It can be worked in many ways: Succeeding rows can repeat the zigzag or oppose it; space between the rows may be varied.

1. Begin on left; holding need horizontally, work four stitches (each below the last, one on each reed) with thread above needle. On fifth stitch, hold thread below needle and then work stitches upward; reverse position of thread and stitches on the fifth stitch; continue in this manner.

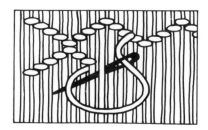

Diamond lattice stitch

Rows may exactly repeat each other, or be reversed to form the lattice.

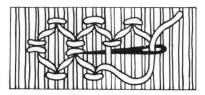

Stem stitch (outline stitch)

Excellent for controlling gathers close to where a band of smocking fits into a yoke or band of fabric.

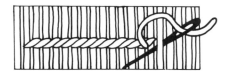

Surface honeycomb stitch

STENCILING FABRIC

1. Never use water with fabric paint—it will run.

2. When mixing colors with white, put white on palette first, and then add tiny dashes of color until you achieve desired shade.

3. Be sure brush is clean and dry. When washing brush between colors, dry thoroughly with paper towel before using again. Stencil lightest colors first. Work one color at a time, rinsing brush thoroughly with water and drying brush completely between colors.

4. Dip just flat tip of brush straight down into paint; blot tip of brush on folded paper towel until bristles are almost dry.

5. Apply paint in appropriate area of stencil, using a circular stroke, or dabbing flat tip of brush directly against fabric Start painting on edge of stencil cutout and work towards center.

STRETCHING FABRIC OR CANVAS ON A FRAME

Most needlework is easier and better if the background fabric or canvas is stretched taut on a frame. There are various types available—ready-made ring frames with stands and supports that allow you to work with both hands free, hand-held ring frames and square frames made of artist's stretcher strips.

Ring frame

1. First remove outer hoop of frame. Lay material over inner ring with part of design to be worked exposed in center. Tighten screw of outer hoop (before placing it in position), adjusting so that it fits down over both inner ring and material very snugly. Do not press hoop all the way down; just push it on so that it fits firmly all around.

2. Pull fabric taut while simultaneously pressing down on rim of frame with palms. Work around the perimeter in this way until material is stretched like a drumskin. Finally, press down outer hoop; it need not be absolutely flat as long as material is taut.

3. Always keep the same hand underneath the frame and pass needle vertically through fabric to other hand on top. Continue, passing needle back and forth vertically in this way, never changing position of your hands.

4. To remove hoop, press down on embroidery with your thumbs, simultaneously lifting off hoop with fingers. Do not attempt to alter screw adjustment before removing hoop.

Stretcher strip frame

1. Wooden stretcher strips of any length with ready-made corner joints are available in art supply stores. Fit four strips of desired length together at corners to form rectangle; make sure corners are at right angles.

2. Lay fabric or canvas in rough position over frame, lining up straight grain of fabric with right angles of frame. Using thumbtacks or staplegun, tack fabric to center of side edge of one stretcher; pulling fabric taut, tack to center of opposite side edge; repeat on remaining two sides.

3. Pulling fabric taut, tack in same manner near one corner, then opposite corner; repeat. Continue tacking fabric around frame in this manner, fastening between previous tacks, until tacks are about ½" apart .

4. To remove fabric from frame, carefully pry up tacks or staples one at a time. Stretchers can be reused.

ENLARGING DESIGNS

1. Each design which must be enlarged is shown with a grid. Take a square piece of tracing paper (it must be exactly square); accurately fold and crease it into smaller squares (folding in

half and half again, etc.). Unfold; if you like, draw lines to delineate the creased squares; refer to the gridded design and copy it in larger scale.

2. Needlepoint or cross-stitch designs may be enlarged and traced down to fabric or canvas, or simply worked straight from the chart, as you prefer.

3. An increasingly available, quick and inexpensive alternative to enlarging your own designs is having them blown up on a photocopier. If you are unsure of the finished size you want for your project, have the design copied this way in several different sizes.

4. Another alternative is an opaque projector, available at art supply or photographic stores. The projector throws a shadow of your design on the wall, larger or smaller according to distance design is placed from projector. Tape canvas or fabric to the wall and trace enlarged design directly onto it.

TRANSFERRING DESIGNS

Preparing fabric

1. Cut fabric so that the selvages run vertically from top to bottom of design, not across. All woven fabric consists of warp (vertical base threads that parallel selvages) and woof (horizontal threads woven across). Warp threads are necessarily stronger; they should run up and down on a picture or a chair seat so that they will take the most strain.

2. Always work on square or rectangular piece of fabric; cut it to shape after needlework is finished (cutting to shape in advance might necessitate cutting lines on the diagonal, which makes fabric pull out of shape easily). Allow plenty of extra fabric for mounting and blocking. However expensive, it is cheap when compared to your work—you can cut away excess easily, but adding on is very difficult!

3. Find center of material: Fold in half vertically down center; repeat horizontally. Mark crease lines by running hard pencil lightly between threads of canvas, or by basting lines on fabric. Repeat this on paper pattern—when transferring design, align lines to keep design centered and square.

4. Edge fabric to prevent fraying while you work: Cover edges with masking tape, or hem or oversew it all around.

Back-lighting

(Medium-weight linen or cotton, delicate fabrics and blends)

1. Stretch fabric onto artist's stretcher strips (see p. 126). With masking tape,

hold boldly traced design close against reverse side of fabric, making sure design is centered and squared with grain of material. Arrange goose-necked lamp behind stretcher frame, maneuvering light so that clear silhouette of design shines through fabric. Trace pattern with fine-tipped permanent marker.

2. Using a light box is another method of back lighting. A light box is easy to make: It's simply an open box containing an electric light, covered by a sheet of frosted Plexiglas. It helps if the sides of the box are cut down slightly toward the front to provide a slanted work surface. Tape both design and fabric on top of lit surface; trace illuminated design.

Basting

(Boldweave textured fabrics and wool; toweling, high-pile fabrics and knits; delicate fabrics and blends)

1. Buy some batiste, organdy, chiffon or crinoline and trace design onto it, using a hard pencil. Pin material with design to reverse side of material to be embroidered, then baste all around the outlines with small running stitches, using a contrasting color thread. The design will then be transferred onto the right side, and may be embroidered right over the running stitches to cover them (you may prefer to draw out the basting stitches later).

Carbon paper

(Medium-weight linen or cotton)

1. Use only dressmaker's carbon (ordinary carbon will smudge)—blue carbon for light materials, white for dark. Establish center of fabric by folding in half and half again. Crease firmly to mark folds, then open fabric. Using masking tape, secure on all four sides to a very smooth, hard work surface. Fold design into four equal parts, upen it up and lay it on top, aligning fold lines of design and fabric.

2. Slide sheet of carbon paper face down between paper and fabric. Anchor paper with heavy weights (books, paperweights, etc.—using weights works better than taping design down, because you can check to see how the carbon is transferring). Trace design with pencil, pressing heavily and drawing in smooth, flowing lines.

Graphs

(Canvas and even-weave fabrics)

1. Geometric designs do not have to be applied; they are counted directly from a graph onto plain canvas or

fabric. Always begin in middle and work out to edges, so that repeat pattern will be balanced and identical on both sides. Always count threads of canvas, never holes. This makes it much less confusing when deciding on size of each stitch and keeps your counting consistent—one square of graph represents one stitch on canvas. To mark edges of design it is not necessary to rule lines; simply draw a pencil between threads of canvas in same way you marked the center.

2. To start a geometric design, pick the predominant pattern and work all of this framework first. Keep checking by running your needle along threads of canvas to make sure that repeats are lined up correctly. Then if you have made a mistake in the count of the framework you will not have so much to unpick as if you had filled in an entire section. Also, once framework is made, you do not have to count threads; you can fill in areas within pattern, using outlines as a guide.

Net method

(Medium-weight linen or cotton; bold-weave textured fabrics and wool)

1. Trace or draw design on paper. Lay piece of net, lawn, tulle or crinoline over drawing; tape down to prevent slipping. With broad felt-tipped permanent marker, trace design onto net.

2. Lay net on top of fabric; tape in position. Once more, outline design with broad-tipped pen. Marker penetrates net and shows through on fabric quite clearly (if background fabric is dark, you may have to touch up faint lines after removing net; if fabric is light, test first to see that marker is not leaving too heavy a line).

Tailor's chalk

(Medium-weight linen or cotton, bold-weave textured fabrics and wool)

1. Available in assorted colors, as pencils or in blocks, tailor's chalk is excellent for drawing a design freehand on fabric. Start with a simple outline; as you work, it is easy to add more detail. If you make a mistake, the chalk easily rubs out.

Trace Erase™ pen

1. This marking pen transfers with a blue line that can be erased by touching it with cold water. It is ideal for freehand drawing because unwanted lines will completely disappear after the needlework is complete. Never apply heat before removing the blue lines or they will become permanent.

Tracing

(Canvas and even-weave fabrics; organdy and transparent fabrics)

1. For canvas and even-weave fabrics, draw design on paper with India ink or permanent, waterproof black felt-tipped marker. Lay on a table or firm surface; hold in position with masking tape. If design is drawn on tracing paper or acetate, place several layers of white paper beneath to make lines more distinct.

2. Establish center of canvas and design. You may find that center lines on canvas, although marked by thread, are not entirely straight, because canvas has been pulled slightly out of shape by storage. Just pull opposite corners and stretch it a little until center lines are at true right angles again. Then when you lay it on top of design, it will lie flat and mesh will be square.

3. Trace design on canvas, using permanent, waterproof black marker or fine paintbrush and India ink. Test pen first—if lines are not waterproof, ink will run during washing and blocking. Draw design with fine, light line (heavy lines are hard to cover with light colors).

Draw as you would on paper, ignoring mesh of canvas and making smooth, flowing lines (you will better interpret a curved shape with your needle if you draw it smoothly on the canvas rather than simplifying it with a zigzag along the meshes).

4. For organdy and transparent fabrics, prepare fabric and design; tape design to smooth surface; tape fabric on top, making sure it is square (it is apt to stretch). Using a hard "H" pencil, lightly trace design. A hard pencil is better than pen or brush on delicate fabrics. Keep lines suitably light so that they will be completely covered by the fine stitching.

Transfer pencil

(Medium-weight linen or cotton)

1. Available in most needlework stores, hectograph transfer pencil is a speedy method useful for bold designs on washable fabric. Using pink transferring pencil, outline design on layout or tracing paper, then turn face downward and iron it on fabric, using iron set for cotton. Lift and press iron—do not rub, since this might move paper pattern and cause smudging. Broad pink line provided by this method may be washed out when embroidery is finished.

Waste canvas

(Medium-weight linen or cotton; bold-weave textured fabrics and wool, toweling, high-pile fabrics and knits; delicate fabrics and blends)

Waste canvas is a thin openweave scrim available by the yard. It is used for transferring geometric designs in cross stitch onto any fabric that does not have a clearly defined weave, such as muslin or organdy.

1. Baste waste canvas over whole area where pattern is to be. Stretch material and canvas in embroidery frame and stitch pattern through both thicknesses, keeping stitches even by counting threads of canvas. Whe design is finished, unravel threads of canvas at edges and draw them out, one by one. If fabric is washable, it may be easier to do this if you first soak the embroidery in cold water; this softens the sizing in the canvas and loosens the threads enough to allow them to slip out easily.

Suppliers

Antoon J. Khouri
31 Twitchel Street
Wellesley, MA 02181
(*Bride's hankies and baby's bonnet sets made up*)

CM Offray & Son, Inc.
Box 601, Route 24
Chester, NJ 07930
(*Ribbon designs*)

Erica Wilson Needleworks*
717 Madison Avenue
New York, NY 10021
(*Trace Erase™ pen, canvas by the yard, needles, crewel wool, embroidery floss*)

Husqvanna/Viking Sewing Machine Co., Inc.
2300 Louisiana Avenue North
Minneapolis, MN 55427-3666
(*Machine for embroidery*)

Illinois Bronze Paint Co.
300 East Main Street
Lake Zurich, IL 60047
(*Fabric paint*)

Joan Toggitt
35 Fairfield Place
West Caldwell, NJ 07006
(*Fabrics for cross stitch: Aida cloth, etc.*)

Little Miss Muffet
316 Nancy Lynn Lane
Knoxville, TN 37919
(*gathering machine for smocking*)

M & J Trimming Co.
1008 Sixth Avenue
New York, NY 10018
(*Sewing and embroidery materials*)

Nice Aroma
P.O. Box 5028
Spartanburg, SC 29304
(*Dyed and accented rice for stuffing pillows, etc.*)

Simplicity Pattern Co.
200 Madison Avenue
New York, NY 10016
(*Bridal dress patterns*)

Stacey Fabrics Corp.
38 Passaic Street
Woodridge, NJ 07075
(*Trace Erase™ fabric*)

Vogue/Butterick Co.
161 Avenue of the Americas
New York, NY 10013
(*Bridal dress patterns*)
If you have any questions about a Vogue/Butterick pattern, please call the Vogue/Butterick Consumer Hotline at (800) 221-2670. [In New York, call (212) 620-2531] You may also write to Vogue/Butterick at the above address.

Wrights
1 Penn Plaza
New York, NY 10001
(*Lace*)

The following projects are available as kits from Erica Wilson Needleworks:

Country Bride Quilt (p. 10)
Monograms and Birthday Flowers (p. 14)
Wildflower & Lace Pillow (p. 17)
Code Flag Belt (p. 20)
Needlepoint Slippers (p. 20)
Bride's Hanky/Christening Bonnet (p. 27)
Embroidered Organdy Tablecloth (p. 28)
Smocked Dress (p. 30)
Welcome Mat (p. 44)
Needlepoint Rose-Covered Cottage (p. 50)
Swan Pillow (p. 51)
Crewel Roses (p. 52)
Victorian Roses Needlepoint Rug (p. 53)
Valentine's Day Cross-Stitch Bunny Heart (p. 58)
Thanksgiving Trapunto Pillow (p. 62)
Anniversary Sampler (p. 63)